Joseph Firth Bottomley Firth

London Government, and How to Reform It

Joseph Firth Bottomley Firth

London Government, and How to Reform It

ISBN/EAN: 9783337297312

Printed in Europe, USA, Canada, Australia, Japan

Cover: Foto ©Suzi / pixelio.de

More available books at **www.hansebooks.com**

LONDON GOVERNMENT,

AND

HOW TO REFORM IT.

BY

J. F. B. FIRTH, LL.B., M.P.,

PRESIDENT OF THE LONDON MUNICIPAL REFORM LEAGUE.

REPRINTED BY PERMISSION OF THE COBDEN CLUB.

"A digest of anarchy."—BURKE.

London:

THE LONDON MUNICIPAL REFORM LEAGUE,
4, LANCASTER HOUSE, SAVOY, STRAND.
KERBY & ENDEAN, 440, OXFORD STREET.
1882.

UNWIN BROTHERS, LITTLE BRIDGE STREET, 71A, LUDGATE HILL, E.C.

PREFACE.

THE following Essay was written at the request of the Cobden Club, and is published by them in their work on "Local Government and Taxation in the United Kingdom, 1882." It had been my intention to write a text-book for the use of the London Municipal Reform League during the winter campaign of 1880, and the suggestion of the Cobden Club, although somewhat delaying the publication, has ensured a wider circle of readers outside London.

Since the autumn of 1880, when this Paper was written, the question of London Government has assumed an immediate importance not then contemplated; and the contest as to the necessity for reform has been displaced by arguments as to the shape such reform ought to take. The principle of a representative municipal authority finally controlling all expenditure and all administration, will be found fully discussed in the following pages. This principle has now been confirmed and accepted, both by the Government and by the inhabitants of London.

PREFACE.

Provided such an authority be constituted, the details of local administration are, in my judgment, of comparative unimportance. I adhere to the views on this matter which were elaborated in my work on London Government six years ago, but I have in the present Paper indicated a method of constituting local authorities which may possibly meet the views of many persons who consider local assistance to be of first importance, and which at the same time preserves intact the necessary principle of a complete and unified representative control.

NEW COURT, TEMPLE,
    February 21*st*, 1882.

CONTENTS.

	PAGE
Municipal Reform not granted to London : reason for this	9
Unsuccessful attempts at Reform	10
Further attempts at Reform	10
Abandonment of question by Government	11
Recent propositions for London Reform	11
THE CORPORATION OF THE CITY OF LONDON :—	12
The Lord Mayor	13
Functions, &c., of the Lord Mayor	13
The Liverymen Franchise	13
Aldermen of the City of London	14
Control of the Guilds by Aldermen	15
The Recorder	15
The Common Serjeant, &c.	16
Judicial Elections	16
Magistracy of Aldermen	16
Aldermen at Central Criminal Court	16
Brokers' rents	17
Common Council	17
Representation	17
Committees of the Common Council	18
Advantages of City Committees	18
Irish Society	18
Commission of Sewers	19
Functions of Commission of Sewers	19
City Lands and Bridge House Estates Committees	20
Gresham Committee	20
Coal and Wine Dues	20
Produce of Coal and Wine Dues	21
Grain Duty	21

CONTENTS.

	PAGE
Market Jurisdiction of the City	22
City Opposition to new Markets	23
London Food Supply under a Central Body	23
Billingsgate Market	23
Action of Common Council in matter	24
City Schools	24
City Courts	25
City Police	25
Royal Hospitals	26
The Chamberlain	26
The Remembrancer, Town Clerk, &c.	26
Income from City Estate	26
Capital Income on City Estate	27
Other City Accounts	27
Total Income and Expenditure	27
Loan Liability	27
No independent Audit	28
Court of Common Hall	28
Municipal Rights of Liverymen	29
Liverymen under new Corporation	29
Origin of City Guilds	29
Former Character of Guilds	30
Charters of the Guilds	30
Rights of Crown and City over Guilds	31
New Charters in 1684	31
Charters of City of London	32
Method of dealing with Charters	33
Legal effect of Charters	33
Confirmation of Charters	34
The *Quo Warranto:* its effect	34
City Charters at the Revolution	35
THE METROPOLITAN BOARD OF WORKS:—	36
Metropolis Management Act, 1855	37
Constitution of Board	37
Representation at the Board	37
Sewerage Jurisdiction of Board	38
Drainage System under new Corporation	38
River Embankments and Floods Prevention	39
Bridges	39
Bridges, Embankments, &c., under new Corporation	40
Street Improvements	40
Street Improvements under new Corporation	41
Parks, Commons, and Open Spaces	41
Parks, &c., under new Corporation	42

CONTENTS.

	PAGE
Fire Brigade	42
Inadequacy of present System	43
American System	44
Work of Fire Brigade	44
Jurisdiction of M.B.W. under Building Acts	44
Further Building Jurisdiction	45
System of Building Control	45
Naming of Streets	45
Minor Jurisdictions of the Metropolitan Board	46
Explosive Substances	47
Petroleum	47
Dairy Inspection, &c.	47
Diseases of Animals	47
Infant Protection	48
Minor Jurisdictions under new Corporation	48
Artizans' Dwellings	48
Accommodation for dispossessed Poor	49
City Funds and the London Poor	49
Metropolitan Board : Method of Work	50
Municipal Patriotism of Board	50
Rateable Value of the Metropolis	51
Loan Liability of Board	51
Loans to Local Authorities	51
Metropolitan Board: Capital Expenditure	52
Current Expenditure	52
Repayment of Debt	53
Metropolitan Stock	53
Net Current Expenditure	53
Total Income and Expenditure	53
VESTRIES AND DISTRICT BOARDS :—	54
Divisions of London for Local Government	54
Vestry Jurisdictions	55
Dust Removal	55
Dust Removal under new Corporation	55
Paving, Watering, Cleansing	55
Defects of present Street Control	56
Street Watering and Cleansing	56
Street Paving at present and under new Corporation	57
Uniform Street Control	58
Surface and Subterranean Street Control	58
Minor Vestry Jurisdictions	59
Medical Officers	59
Rates	60
Local Taxation	60

CONTENTS.

	PAGE
Baths and Wash-houses	61
Mortuaries, Adulteration Acts, &c.	61
Tramway Jurisdiction now and under new Corporation	62
Ecclesiastical Jurisdiction	62
Vestry Elections	63
Burial Boards	63
Vestries and District Boards: Income and Expenditure	64
Loans	64
Audit of Vestry Accounts	64
Vestry Reports	64
Metropolitan Boundary	65
"CORPORATION" OF WESTMINSTER:—	65
"City" of Westminster	66
Former Divisions and Jurisdictions	66
Members and Officers of "Corporation"	67
Income of "Corporation" of Westminster	67
TOWER OF LONDON:—	68
Present Jurisdiction	68
COUNTY JURISDICTIONS IN LONDON:—	68
Sheriffwicks	69
County Jurisdictions under new Corporation	69
SCHOOL BOARD FOR LONDON:—	69
Class of Members	70
Number of Children and School Provision	70
Buildings, Character of Teaching, &c.	71
Cost	72
School Attendance, &c.	72
Details of School Board Work and Management	73
Income and Expenditure of School Board	74
Loan Liability of School Board	74
School Board under Municipal System	75
Utilization of Endowments	75
Endowments under new Corporation	76
POOR LAW ADMINISTRATION IN LONDON:—	77
Metropolitan Common Poor Fund	77
Poor Relief: Indoor and Outdoor Relief	78
Statistics of London Pauperism	78
Metropolitan Asylums Board	78
Income and Expenditure of Metropolitan Asylums Board	79
Central Control of Poor Law System	80
Ultimate Transfer of Boards of Guardians to new Corporation	80
Final Control by new Corporation	81

CONTENTS. vii

	PAGE
Result of Central Control	81
Registration Returns	81
METROPOLITAN POLICE:—	82
Necessity of Uniform Police System	82
Present Control	83
Principle applicable to Control of Police	84
Police under new Corporation	84
Metropolitan Police District	85
City Police: Cost	85
Metropolitan Police: Cost	85
Strength and Work of Police Force	85
LONDON CABS:—	86
Hardships of existing Law	86
Control of Locomotion under new Corporation	87
THAMES CONSERVANCY BOARD:—	87
Constitution of Board	88
Nature of River Control	88
Income and Expenditure: Lower Navigation	89
Income and Expenditure: Upper Navigation	89
LEA CONSERVANCY BOARD:—	90
Lea Conservancy: Income and Expenditure	90
Rivers Conservancy under new Corporation	90
LONDON WATER SUPPLY:—	91
Sources of Supply	91
Nature of Supply	91
Amount of Supply	92
Unsuitability of Supply	92
Cost of new Supply	93
Water Trust Bill of 1880	93
Select Committee on Water Supply, 1880	94
Water Trust: Difficulty of Constitution	95
Water Supply under new Corporation	95
Water Companies: Income and Expenditure	96
LONDON GAS SUPPLY:—	96
Gas Act of 1860	97
Action of Corporation of London	97
Unjustifiable Action of Metropolitan Board	98
City of London Gas Act	99
Present Conditions of London Gas Supply	99
Gas Supply under a new Corporation	100
Gas Companies' Income and Expenditure	100
Gas Companies' Capital Account	101

	PAGE
CONSIDERATION OF REFORM :—	102
Grouping of Jurisdictions	102
Effect of Recent Legislation	102
Vestry Jurisdictions under new Corporation	103
Jurisdictions requiring Change	103
Argument for a Single Central Authority	104
Opinion of Commissioners of 1837 and 1854	104
Mr. Ayrton's Committee	106
Argument from Recent Legislation	106
Separate Municipalities	106
Objections to Single Municipality	107
Objection to Magnitude	108
Methods of Creation : Municipality Bill of 1880 : Details of Bill	108
Procedure of Municipality under Bill of 1880	109
Methods of Creation : Adaptation of existing Systems	109
Extension of Corporation of City of London	110
Character of City Institutions	110
Amalgamation of Board of Works and City	110
Committee Amalgamation	111
Retention of City Committees	111
Facility of Transition	112
Power of complete Internal Reform	112
Area of new Corporation	113
Division of Area in Bill of 1880	113
Temporary acceptance of existing Areas	113
Division of Representation in existing Areas	114
Special Treatment of City	115
Day Census of City	116
Misleading Character of Day Census	117
Numbers of new Corporation	117
Aldermen of new Corporation	118
How to deal with existing Vestries	118
Disadvantage of complete Extinction of Vestries	119
Disadvantages of Local independent Councils	119
Local Councils as part of new Corporation	120
Numbers and Functions of Local Councils	120
Ultimate Functions of Local Councils	121
Election of Municipal Councillors, &c.	121
Tenure of Office	122
Suggested Method of Election of Aldermen, Councillors, &c.	122
Case for Reform	123
Future of London under Unified Municipal System	124
Conclusion	124

LONDON GOVERNMENT, AND HOW TO REFORM IT.

By J. F. B. Firth, Esq., L.L.B., M.P.

It may be doubted whether, amongst the many important measures of beneficent legislation enacted during the present century, there is any one which has proved more completely advantageous to the people affected by it than the Municipal Corporations Act, 1835. Shortly after the passing of this measure, an attempt was made to obtain for the Capital the same rights of local self-government which had been by this Act conceded to the rest of the important towns in the kingdom. A Bill for this purpose, and which would probably have been framed on the same general lines as the Municipal Corporations Act, was repeatedly promised, but never introduced. This was in the first place due to delay on the part of the Municipal Commissioners in the presentation of their report; in the second place—after the presentation of such report—it was due to the vigorously hostile action of the Corporation of the City, who were able, by taking advantage of the exigencies of the party in power, to prevent its introduction. It was not contended that the City in its government was above reproach, or that London beyond its gates was undeserving of municipal institutions. Civic hostility to reform was dictated only by the motive of self-preservation. Glorying in a great historic position, and in the possession of rights and privileges more extended than those of any corporate town in the kingdom, they were anxious and determined to preserve these, and to preserve their vast corporate possessions for their own use alone, without permitting any share to be granted therein to the misgoverned millions outside. The opposition of vested City interests was successful in 1837, and has been successful, in the years that

Municipal Reform not granted to London: reason for this.

have since passed, in preventing the extension of self-governing institutions to the inhabitants of the metropolis.

<small>Unsuccessful attempts at Reform.</small> It is true that in 1855 an Act was passed known as the Metropolis Local Management Act, whereby the Metropolitan Board, the Vestries, and District Boards were constituted; but, as will be hereafter shown, these bodies can lay no claim to be representative municipal institutions. It is also true that, after the presentation of the report of the Commissioners appointed in 1853 to enquire into the Corporation of London, the Administration introduced, in successive years, no less than four measures providing for internal City reforms. But, in one way or another, the City defeated them all. The Bills made provision for only a few of the reforms advocated by the Commissioners, but they were assailed with the most violent opposition. Sir George Grey's Bill of 1856 had to be withdrawn in consequence of a pressure for delay to which that minister expressed himself compelled to yield. The Bill of 1858, contested by the City representatives at every stage, was ultimately referred to a select committee. After the committee had reported, the City petitioned in favour of re-opening the whole question on the basis of allegations which Sir George Grey himself asserted to be deliberately false; and, by a system of prolonged debate and concerted delay on the part of the City representatives, this Bill was also lost.

<small>Further attempts at Reform.</small> Bills introduced in 1859 and 1860 suffered the same fate. Each successive measure was weaker than the one which preceded it; and Sir George Lewis's Bill of 1860 was almost valueless. In 1863 Sir George Grey attempted to deal with one only of the many reforms recommended by the Commissioners, and to amalgamate the City and Metropolitan police; but, as the City Police Bill had been a private measure, the City took exception to the non-publication of November notices, and the Government bill was thrown out as not having complied with the standing orders of the House of Commons. Speaking on this measure, Sir

George Grey testified that, whenever he had touched "any question which affected the alleged rights and privileges of the City, a power of resistance was shown which it was difficult to estimate too highly."

In 1861 and 1867 two committees of the House of Commons, appointed at the instance of Mr. Ayrton, inquired into and reported upon the system of local government and taxation in the metropolis, but no legislation resulted. The services rendered by Mr. Ayrton on these Committees and in other ways to the cause of London Reform were of great value. But since 1863 no responsible government has ventured to approach the question of City reform, and yet no question has been more urgently demanding solution. Introducing the Municipal Corporations Bill, Lord John Russell truly stated "that existing municipal corporations neither possess, nor deserve, the confidence of His Majesty's subjects," and said that it was not the intention of the Government to stop short in this matter at Temple Bar. Lord Brougham recalled these professions when addressing the House of Lords a few years later, and observed, "If the smaller corporations throughout the country needed reform, I will maintain that the Metropolitan Corporation requires it a great deal more, and is, in its various departments, entirely deserving of the name heretofore given it of the giant abuse of that class." A few of the prominent evils then existing in the City Corporation have been removed; but in other respects its condition has altered for the worse; and it remains to-day the most remarkable illustration of how a powerful and united vested interest can successfully delay the most needed reform, even when such delay works the denial of common municipal rights to millions of people.

Abandonment of question by Government.

Several attempts have been made in recent years by private members of Parliament to introduce municipal government into London. In 1867 and 1868 Mr. Stuart Mill introduced Bills for this purpose. The first was withdrawn, the second

Recent propositions for London Reform.

defeated through City agency upon the standing orders. In 1869 and 1870 Mr. Buxton re-introduced similar measures. The Bills of 1869 were withdrawn on the assurance that the question would receive the consideration of the Government. The Bills of 1870 were referred to a select committee, and so shelved. Two of the Bills proposed the erection of London into a single county, and the establishment of a central metropolitan corporation, to consist of 212 persons, variously elected. A third Bill provided for the constitution of nine municipal boroughs, to whom the powers of the vestries were to be transferred. In 1875 a Bill was introduced by Lord Elcho and Sir Ughtred Kay-Shuttleworth for the establishment of a single municipal government. It did not, however, reach the second reading. In 1878 Sir Ughtred Kay-Shuttleworth again brought the anomalies of existing systems very forcibly before the House of Commons. Towards the close of the session of 1880 another Bill was prepared and introduced for the same purpose. Both these latter measures served the purpose of presenting complete schemes of reform, but the subject is one that, from its magnitude and complexity, must necessarily be undertaken by a responsible government.

We shall proceed to examine the present conditions of London government, and, at the same time, to discuss the manner in which the various branches of municipal work may be most usefully performed. We shall then indicate the method in which a uniform and representative system may be established.

THE CORPORATION OF THE CITY OF LONDON.

The only municipal government in London is the Corporation of the City. This Corporation is one of the oldest in the kingdom. It differs in many important respects from other corporations, and, although possessing a complete power of internal reform, still retains customs and jurisdictions inconsistent with the principles of the Municipal Corporations Act, 1835, and unequivocally condemned by more than one Parliamentary commission. The head of the Corporation and the chief magistrate of the City is the Lord Mayor. He is the modern representative of the Port-gerefa, or Port-reeve, who, under Norman kings, presided at the folk-mote, and over the great hustings-court of the city. In pursuance of a custom more than 600 years old, each Lord Mayor is presented to the Lord Chancellor in order to receive the Royal assent to his appointment, and takes the oath of office before the judges at Westminster. The form of his election has repeatedly changed; —at the present time he is selected from City Aldermen who have served the office of Sheriff. The custom is for the Liverymen of the various City guilds to meet at the Guildhall on the 29th of September to nominate two Aldermen, one of whom is afterwards selected as Lord Mayor by the general body of Aldermen. Practically the senior Alderman who has not passed the chair is almost invariably chosen as Lord Mayor.

The Lord Mayor.

The Lord Mayor of London is Lord Lieutenant within the City, and chief depositary of its privileges. He is a judge at the Central Criminal Court, a justice of the peace, and the *ex-officio* chairman of the Court of Aldermen, the Court of Common Council, and the Court of Common Hall. He is a member of the Privy Council, is Chief Butler at the Coronation, and the chief dispenser of the hospitality of the City. He is provided with a chaplain and a complete staff of officers suitable for his position. He has an allowance out of the City cash of £10,000 for his ordinary expenses during the year, in addition to which the City paid, during the year 1880, more than £6,000 for expenses in connection with the mayoralty; he has a regal coach, and the user of some £40,000 worth of plate. He is not, however, expected to defray the cost of all civic hospitality out of so small a sum as £10,000 a year. Upon the occasion of the visits of foreign monarchs, or of members of the Royal Family, the City defrays the cost of entertainment out of its own public funds.

Functions, &c., of the Lord Mayor.

The election of the Lord Mayor and other City officers by the Liverymen of the City guilds is the most absurd and

The Liverymen franchise.

anachronous franchise existing in any corporate city in the world. Four hundred years ago all the Liverymen were traders carrying on business within the City; to-day they have in many cases no connection with the City whatever; and the Commissioners of 1837 say, " We cannot discover, in the constitution or practice of the governing bodies, any single circumstance which shows, or even probably suggests, the propriety of their being fixed upon for the responsible office of selecting the electors for the high offices of the Corporation." The Commissioners of 1854 strongly endorsed this opinion, and they recommended that the Lord Mayor should be elected by the Common Council. If a general London Municipality be established, he may be usefully so elected from amongst the whole body of citizens. If such new corporation were constructed on the principle of extending the City over the Metropolis, the new Lord Mayor would at first retain the present functions of the City Mayor, except those which are connected with the administration of justice.

Aldermen of the City of London. There are twenty-six aldermen in the City of London, representing as many wards. It is not necessary that an alderman should reside within the City, and the number of people whom he represents is in some wards exceedingly small. Thus, an alderman elected for Queenhithe Ward in 1880 had only 273 constituents, and two other present aldermen received, in contested elections, only 163 and 121 votes respectively. Immediately upon his election an alderman of London becomes a magistrate for life; and, in the course of a few years, as Lord Mayor claims at home and abroad to be the representative of the municipal institutions of the whole metropolis. For several hundred years the aldermen have possessed legislative functions through "the Court of Mayor and Aldermen in the Inner Chamber." This Court elects the Recorder, the Steward of Southwark, and other officers of the Corporation. It is the bench of magistrates and the licensing authority of the City; it admits brokers; has a certain control over City cash, over the police force, and some other matters; it also possesses a full control over the rulers of Livery companies, and over their internal regulations.

As every City alderman is also the Liveryman of a City guild, and as most of the City guilds have long since departed from their original purpose, the Court of Aldermen has ceased to exercise this jurisdiction. But the City has often claimed, by virtue of Royal charter, that its customs, rights, and privileges survive, whether used, not used, or even abused. These inherent rights would therefore remain, and, in the hands of a council elected from the whole metropolis, may prove of much utility. But the Court of Aldermen still claim and still exercise the right to grant powers to the Livery companies to increase their livery—that is to say, to increase the number of persons who, by payment of a sum of money, may purchase the right to enjoy the endowments of a trade association, to vote in the election of City officers, and in the election of Members of Parliament. If a central council be constituted for the whole of London, or the City Corporation extended so as to include the metropolitan area, it will be necessary, either in the constituting Act or subsequently, to abolish the Court of Aldermen and transfer some of its functions to the central council. *Control of the Guilds by Aldermen.*

The Recorder of London is appointed by the Court of Aldermen. The office is worth £3,000 a year. The Recorder is a justice of the peace, a judge at the Central Criminal Court, and a judge in civil cases in the Mayor's Court. He is described in the *Liber Albus*, written in 1419, as one of the most expert and able apprentices of the law in the whole City, and the men selected have generally reflected honour on the Court and the Corporation. The office, being a judicial one, ought no longer to remain the subject of election, but should be placed in the nomination of the Secretary of State, as in other towns. *The Recorder.*

The Deputy-Recorder, or Common Serjeant, who is sworn in

The Common Serjeant, &c.

Judicial elections.

Magistracy of Aldermen.

Aldermen at Central Criminal Court.

before the Court of Aldermen, is subject to election at the hands of the Court of Common Council. The appointment to this office ought also to be placed in the hands of the Crown. So also with the post of judge of the City of London Court. This appointment, like that of Common Serjeant, is the result of a successful canvass of the Common Council. Speaking of this matter in the House of Lords forty years ago, Lord Brougham said, "Where is the decency of a judge who is to take his seat on the bench of justice, who is to be clothed with the ermine of the law, and who is to administer justice in the capital of the country to two millions of Her Majesty's subjects, being chosen by election after a canvass?"

The magistracy of aldermen should also be abolished, and stipendiary magistrates should be appointed within the City. Speaking of the administration of justice by City aldermen, Lord Brougham said, "I complain of the administration of justice in the City of London, and I bring it before your lordships that you may pronounce sentence against it, and that that grievous abuse, which by a perversion is often called the administration of justice in the City, may cease." Since Lord Brougham thus spoke of it, the administration of justice by City aldermen has certainly not improved, and is not infrequently productive of grave scandal, as for example when a year or two ago a City alderman publicly in the Mansion House "impeached" the Lord Mayor, "in the name of the citizens of London, as having brought discredit" on his office, &c. Moreover, to confide important judicial functions in the commercial centre of the world to a body of men devoid of legal training or knowledge, could only be expected to produce the melancholy and helpless results with which the public are but too painfully familiar.

The Commissioners of 1854 not merely recommended the appointment of stipendiary magistrates in the City, but also the exclusion of City aldermen from the Central Criminal Court. Under the law as it now stands, there is nothing to prevent two of these aldermen conducting a trial for murder at the Old Bailey, and it is customary for one alderman to sit with the actual judge in order to form a quorum, under the Central Criminal Court Act. The Court of Aldermen strongly resented the suggestion of the Commissioners of 1854, and resolved that they "willingly acknowledged the advantage they all received from being present at the trials by the learned judges." They thus regard a court in which they are nominally judges as a kind of university for the completion of city tradesmen's education.

The control over brokers might be transferred to the central council, with a view to the examination of the whole question. At present it is little more than nominal. Each London broker pays five pounds per annum to the City, and the receipts from this source in the year 1880 were £8,490. The power claimed by the Court of Aldermen to reject any elected alderman of whom they disapprove—a power which was recently enforced against the elect of the ward of Cheap—is utterly indefensible. <small>Brokers' rents.</small>

The Common Council of the City is composed of 206 councillors and 26 aldermen, making a total of 232. The Court of Common Council is the chief legislative body of the City. It elects most of the Corporation officials, and has unlimited control over the City cash. <small>Common Council.</small>

Twenty-five of the twenty-six City wards are represented in the Corporation by one alderman and a number of councillors, varying from four to sixteen. There is also a ward of Bridge Without, represented by an alderman only. The total census population of the City was, in 1881, 52,276, or just about half what it was two hundred years ago. With a few exceptions, the members of the Common Council are also members of the Livery companies. A very small number of them have residential addresses within the City, and they belong almost exclusively to one class of the commercial community. Whilst the aldermen are elected for life, the members of the Common Council are chosen yearly, on St. Thomas's Day. A <small>Representation.</small>

B

seat at the Common Council is not, however, in any large proportion of cases severely contested..

Committees of the Common Council. The work of the Corporation is mainly done through committees reporting to the Common Council. As a rule these committees meet monthly, but the Commission of Sewers meets fortnightly, and there are special committees and sub-committees. As the numbers of the Common Council are six times larger than the work which it has to do requires, so the committees are sometimes unnecessary, and always too numerous. But in order to distribute the advantages of membership as much as possible it is provided, by Standing Order 61, that no member shall remain more than four years on the chief committees, and, by Standing Order 60, that no chairman of committee shall be eligible for re-election.

Advantages of City Committees. In his ordinary capacity as Common Councilman every member of the Corporation takes part in the sumptuous festivities of the City. In his capacity as a committee-man his arduous labours are soothed by a succession of entertainments at the public expense, under the presidency of the various chairmen. These functionaries invite the members of the committee to dinner, and send in the bills to the Corporation. For the purpose of the entertainment of committees, and for summer excursions for the Common Council, there was paid out of City cash in the year 1880 a sum of between £5,000 and £6,000, being from £20 to £25 per head!

Irish Society. Some of the committees of the Common Council require special mention. The Irish Society is generally regarded as a City committee. It is elected by the Court of Common Council in the month of February. The circumstances of the province of Ulster are greatly changed since King James the First granted to this Society the charter under which they now hold lands in that province. The colonisation of confiscated lands in Ulster was, in 1613, undertaken by the Corporation of the City, acting through this Society. Most of these lands were afterwards divided amongst the Livery companies, who supplied much of the cost, but the Society retained and at present controls various lands, fisheries, and other rights, including municipal rights over the towns of Londonderry and Coleraine, which could not be very well divided. The Society enjoys a large income, exceeding, it is believed, £12,000 a year, part of which is expended in management, and the rest devoted to the benefit of the district. The costs of management include an expensive yearly progress, by the members of the Society, through the north of Ireland. The Commissioners of 1837 say they do not "know of any pretext of argument for continuing the municipal supremacy of the Irish Society." The Municipality of London Bill, 1880, adopting the suggestion of the Commissioners of 1854, provided for the dissolution of the Irish Society, and for the vesting of its property in trustees to be appointed by the Lord Chancellor of Ireland.

The Commission of Sewers consists of 95 members, including the Recorder and Common Serjeant. It has a regulating Act of Parliament of its own, and an elaborate staff of officers. It controls minor drainage, paving, cleansing, lighting, street improvement, nuisances and sanitary matters within the City area, and levies a sewers' and consolidated rate in the City. *Commission of Sewers.*

It is the local authority for buildings in the City; has the functions of a burial board and the control of bake-houses, and other matters. If reform took the shape of the extension of the City Corporation, this committee would assume the central control over the same matters throughout the metropolis, and the various vestries and Board of Works officers now carrying them out would become officers of this committee. The consolidated rate for lighting, cleansing, paving, &c., levied in the City in the year ending September, 1880, was £214,516, and the sewers' rate for minor City drainage, £13,865. City paving cost £30,627; lighting, £14,353; cleansing, £30,074; salaries, £10,978. There is a constant conflict between this committee and the Corporation, owing to the claim to independent powers advanced by the commission. The effect of this was illustrated *Functions of Commission of Sewers.*

in 1881 by a case where the Corporation granted rights over City land after the Commissioners had resolved to take it for improvements, and thus wasted some £8,000 or £10,000.

City Lands and Bridge House Estates Committees. The most important committee of the Common Council is the City Lands' Committee, which has the superintendence of the City Estates. The Bridge House Estates Committee has an analogous control over the estates the income of which is available for the repair of the bridges. The income derived from the Bridge House Estates is applicable to the maintenance of London, Southwark, and Blackfriars Bridges. This income in 1880 was £68,197, of which £64,316 was from rents. The expenditure was £64,025, of which £32,000 was on capital account. The expenditure included the salaries of two Bridge-masters, elected by the livery of the City guilds. The duty of these masters is to watch the fabric of the bridges. One of them is a City tobacconist.

Gresham Committee. The Gresham Estate Committee controls the City's moiety of the noble bequest left by Sir Thomas Gresham for educational purposes. The trust has been seriously mismanaged, and of the income of £7,827 in 1880, only the sum of £504 was devoted to any educational purpose. This sum was expended in the maintenance of evening City lectures on astronomy, music, divinity, and geometry.

Coal and Wine dues. The Coal, Corn, and Finance Committee control and report on matters of City finance, and undertake the collection of the coal and wine dues. In 1694 the City of London obtained power to raise a duty on wine and coal for the purpose of repaying a fund of £750,000, of which they alleged that they had been defrauded during the late reign. The truth of the allegation does not appear to have been satisfactorily established, but by dint of bribing the Speaker of the House of Commons—for accepting which bribe he was afterwards expelled the House—and by other methods, they succeeded in getting a taxing power over coal and wine. All the money has been long since repaid, but the tax proved too useful to be lightly relinquished, and it is still levied. Thirteenpence per ton is levied on all coal coming within fifteen miles of St. Paul's. Of this sum the produce of ninepence, part of the duty, is paid over towards general metropolitan improvements, and the fourpence is paid to the City for City improvements.

The ninepenny coal duty produced in 1880 £330,345. The wine duty produced £10,803. The fourpenny coal duty produced £146,820; making the total produce of the coal and wine dues £487,968. Of this sum £74,264 was allowed as drawback on coal re-exported. The amount paid into the Treasury to the credit of the Thames Embankment and Metropolis Improvement Fund was £279,726. The proportion of the City's fourpence, which was appropriated to payment of interest on Holborn Valley Improvements, was £71,658, and to reduction of loans, £47,223. The rents of the coal market (built out of this tax) produced £1,998, and the cost of maintenance was £2,048. *Produce of the Coal and Wine dues.*

The coal and wine dues (unless renewed by Paliament) come to an end in 1889, and, in whatever manner the money may be raised, there is no doubt that these dues work great injustice. They are unjust to the suburban districts outside London, who are thus compelled to contribute to metropolitan improvements, and the coal dues are especially hard on the poor.

There is also a Metage or Grain Committee. This committee controls the collection of a tax levied by weight on all grain coming into the port of London. The amount received in 1880 was £23,325, and there is a loan liability charged on the fund of nearly £200,000. Prior to 1871 the City claimed a right of compulsory grain metage, but in that year a private Act of Parliament was obtained enabling them to charge by weight. The right of compulsory metage had been contested a few years previously, and the City failed to establish it, but by alleging its continued existence, by changing the charge to one by weight rather than measure, and by offering to exper *Grain duty.*

the produce on Open Spaces, they obtained an Act enabling them to continue to raise a tax on the food of all Londoners. They have expended it in the purchase of West Ham Park, Burnham Beeches, and Epping Forest. The tax is in all respects a most vicious one.

<small>Market Jurisdiction of the City.</small> There are also several Market Committees of the Common Council. The title of the City to its market jurisdiction rests upon charter. The subject is first mentioned in the first charter of Edward the Third, which grants that no market shall be granted by the Crown within seven miles about the City. Confirmed and renewed by succeeding sovereigns, this right was specifically regranted in the great Inspeximus Charter of Charles I. in 1638, whereby it is provided that no market shall be granted, erected, or allowed by the Crown *infra septem leucas in circuitu civitatis*. The City has constantly acted under these charters, and opposed the establishment of markets in London without their consent; and in cases where the City have not opposed, the House of Lords has sometimes required their consent in writing under their common seal to be affixed to a Market Bill before passing it. The result of the action of the City in the question of public markets has been to largely enhance the cost, and limit the supply of food to the metropolis. They claim, under these old charters granted, for a money consideration, the right to tax the food of four millions of Londoners, by compelling them to go to Billingsgate and to Smithfield every day for their supply. The suburban Londoner has to pay the cost of the extra carriage of food in the first instance to the City market, and afterwards by the carts of butcher and fishmonger going and returning from the City. The inhabitants of provincial or continental towns have retail markets near at hand, but no such market can be established in London so long as the City monopoly is permitted to continue. This monopoly has hitherto been defended with the same complete disregard of the public welfare as other City privileges.

An illustration of this may be found in the evidence, reluc- *City opposition to new Markets.* tantly given, to the last City commission by the present City Chamberlain, where he admitted the secret expenditure of £2,750 in opposing a Government bill for removing Smithfield Market. The money was partly expended in paying literary men to write down the government proposition, but chiefly in procuring petitions against the measure from all parts of the country, which were supposed by Parliament to be genuine petitions, but which were really paid for by the City. As the Chamberlain put it, " the expressions of popular opinion are more powerful if the hand is not seen which is moving the agency "—that is to say, if Parliament believes the petitions are genuine it may act upon them.

With an extension of municipal government to the whole *London Food Supply under a Central Body.* of London the question of its food supply may receive full attention; and within a few years the citizens may not merely have the benefit of wholesale and retail markets adequate to their requirements, but also such lower prices for food as will necessarily follow increased facilities for its distribution. In the session of 1881 a power was inserted in the Metropolitan Board of Works Money Bill for the year, enabling that body to enquire into the desirability of establishing markets in London, and to introduce a measure to Parliament. The Board entered on their new duty with light hearts, but soon fell to disagreement amongst themselves as to sites and other matters. Personal interests were made to take precedence of public interests; some of the ardent supporters of a measure became unaccountably its opponents, and eventually the Board resolved to do nothing. A great opportunity was thus given for it to prove itself fit to undertake further duties, or to form the nucleus of a satisfactory government for all London, but the opportunity was deliberately thrown away.

Mr. Spencer Walpole, reporting on Billingsgate in 1881, *Billingsgate Market.* showed how completely it failed in some of the necessary requirements of a market; and, with two-thirds of the fish supply of

London coming by rail, it might be supposed that the necessity for accessible land market accommodation was manifest. But the only solution which many of the City Council regarded as admissible involved the enlargement of Billingsgate at enormous cost. In the course of the discussion of the matter in the Common Council, the leaders of that body repeatedly alleged that this proposal derived its support from a number of men within the Council whose property would be removed if the market were enlarged, and who were anxious to be bought out and compensated from the public purse. The charges did not in anywise astonish or disturb the equanimity of the Common Council of the City of London. That body is too much in the habit of placing personal above public considerations for the accusation to be regarded as a reproach, and no enquiry into its truth was demanded.

Action of Common Council in matter.

It would be only too easy to show how accurately this incident reflects the moving impulse of the Common Council of the City of London, and how necessary it is, even in the interests of public morality, that the whole institution should be reformed. The case for London reform is, however, so strong on its own merits that perhaps we may be excused from undertaking the obnoxious duty. The old oath of a Common Councillor used to run, "that for no favour will you maintain any private profit against the common profit of the City." That test has now been removed, and he is simply required to declare that he will "faithfully perform the duties of the office of a Common Councilman." The elasticity of the modern declaration better fits the situation than the rigidity of the old oath.

City Schools.

The City of London School is under the direct control of a committee of the Corporation. It is nearly a self-supporting institution, the City contribution in 1880 being £2,659, and the scholars' payments £7,847. The Freeman's Orphan School, for the education of children of freemen of the City, involved a charge on the City cash of £5,084. It is also under the management of a committee.

The Law and Parliamentary and City Courts' committee City
has a technical control over the various City Courts. The Courts.
Commissioners of 1837 enumerated fourteen of these Courts
peculiar to the City, and to the Borough of Southwark under
City control. Of these, the Court of the Borough of South-
wark, the Courts of Requests in London and Southwark, the
Court of St. Martin's-le-Grand, the Courts of Conservancy,
Finsbury Court Leets and Court Baron, the Court of the
Manor of Duke's-place, the Court of Pie Poudre, and the
Court of Hustings, are practically obsolete. Of the rest, the
Mayor's Court still flourishes, and the City of London Court
(in which the two courts of the Sheriff's Compter have now
been merged) does probably more work than any other
Court of the kind in existence. The Central Criminal
Court has a jurisdiction wider than the metropolis, but
whilst the Lord Mayor and aldermen are technically judges
of it, their attendance is but nominal, and will come to an
end with any scheme of reform. The Chamberlain has also
a Court, where he is supposed to control unruly City apprentices, and where his jurisdiction extends even to imprisonment in Newgate, but these functions are practically
obsolete.

There is a City Police Committee to control the City police City Police.
force. It is now a very effective body. The total cost of the
force in 1880 to the City was about £100,000. The subject
is further considered hereafter when dealing with metropolitan
police. There are also a General Purposes Committee, a Sanitary
Committee, a Library Committee, a Gas and Water Committee,
an Epping Forest Committee, an Officers and Clerks' Committee,
and several others. The Officers and Clerks' Committee serves
a very useful purpose in considering the functions and emolu-
ments of any office which becomes vacant, with a view to the
Common Council modifying the conditions of its future tenure.
The power of internal regulation possessed by the Common
Council has proved most useful in these matters. The old

Royal Hospitals.

system under which Corporation offices were put up to auction is now removed.

The Court of Common Council, under the provisions of 22 Geo. III., c. 77, appoint 12 governors of St. Bartholomew's Hospital; of Bridewell and Bethlehem Hospitals 12, of Christ's Hospital 12, and of St. Thomas's Hospital 12. The historic connection of the City with these hospitals is a matter of great interest. Many reforms are demanded, especially in Christ's Hospital. In any new scheme the control would be continued to a central authority able to examine into the whole question. The appointments to the office of governor, and the exercise of other patronage over London almshouses, are carefully divided amongst the City wards.

The Chamberlain.

The City Treasurer is known as the Chamberlain. He is the keeper of the elaborate system of accounts prepared every year. The total profits of the office, mainly derived from floating balances in the various City accounts, was, in 1880, £13,008. The expenditure was mainly on account of the staff. The Chamberlain has a salary of £2,500, and also received in 1880 £2,500 additional by way of gratuity for faithful service. It is customary for City officials to petition the Common Council for such recognition.

The Remembrancer, Town Clerk, &c.

The Parliamentary Officer of the City is the Remembrancer. His duty is to watch the interests of the City in Parliament, and by every means to prevent legislation which may prejudicially affect City rights and privileges. This office is now in abeyance, pending the litigation between its nominal holder and the Corporation as to the right of the Common Council to declare the office vacant without assigning cause. The most heinous offence of the Remembrancer, in the eyes of the Common Council, lay in the strenuous endeavour which he made to determine the abuses and corruptions which he found prevalent in his office. There is also a Town Clerk, with a salary of £2,250, an Architect, with a salary of £2,000, a Chief Engineer to the Commissioners of Sewers, with a salary of £2,000, and many other officers. These salaries are often largely augmented.

The current income of the City in the year 1880, from what is termed the City Estate, was £303,137. This included £131,735 from rents and interest; £145,695 from markets at Islington, Smithfield, Leadenhall, Farringdon, and Billingsgate, and various sums from the grain duty, fruit metage, brokers' rents, court fees, and smaller matters. The current expenditure on the same account was £306,804. This included an expenditure on markets of £135,919, on the civil government of the City of £56,508, pensions £11,159, and other matters, all of which are set out in the accounts. *Income from City Estate.*

The capital income on this account is £462,414, chiefly consisting of loans raised, but including an amount of £39,000 from reserve fund in order to meet overdrawn accounts and demands on City cash. The capital expenditure was £455,234, of which £339,600 was for the discharge of loans, and £92,293 for market erection. The total income on City Estate account was thus £765,551, and the total expenditure, £762,038. *Capital Income on City Estate.*

In addition to the "City Estate account" a large number of accounts are separately kept, some of which are termed Accounts connected with the City's Estate, and others Public Trust Funds. They include the accounts of the Bridge House Estates, Gresham Estate, various improvement accounts; Deptford Market accounts; the Coal, Wine and Grain Duty accounts; the various School accounts; the accounts of the Sewers Commission; the Police Rate; Ward Rates; the City Courts, and others; altogether nearly fifty separate accounts. Many of these have large balances in hand, and it is not easy to see why so diffuse a system of book-keeping is adopted, unless it be to make profit out of these balances. Such profit in 1880 amounted to £10,912. Taken as a whole, however, the City accounts are infinitely better presented than those of the Metropolitan Board of Works. *Other City Accounts.*

The total income, capital and current, of these separate accounts was about £1,600,000, and the expenditure nearly the same. The total capital and current income of the City of *Total Income and Expenditure.*

London in 1880 may thus be stated generally at £2,350,000, and the expenditure about the same.

Loan Liability.
The City has a total loan liability of £5,274,800; of this sum £1,671,500 is in respect of the Holborn Valley Improvements. The sale of surplus land may reduce this, and the City's fourpenny coal duty is hypothecated for the same purpose. But in 1889, when the duty comes to an end (and Parliament would never renew it to the present Corporation, if indeed at all), there would, from this account, be an additional charge of at least £40,000 a year on the City Estate; but as that Estate account is already overdrawn the amount would, it is presumed, have to be raised by rates. There is still due on the Islington Market account £400,000, on the Smithfield Markets £1,584,000, on the Deptford Market £259,500, on Billingsgate enlargement £272,000, on the Southwark and Blackfriars Bridge accounts £555,000, on the Grain Duty £199,000, making with some other items the sum previously mentioned. Some of the money is borrowed at $4\frac{1}{4}$ per cent., but most of it is now at 4 or $3\frac{1}{2}$ per cent.

No independent Audit.
There is no independent audit of City accounts. Every year the Common Hall—that is, the body of Liverymen of the Guilds—appoints four persons as auditors, but their duties are merely to examine vouchers. They never surcharge. Hence the City accounts have been disfigured by many unjustifiable items. Its extravagance of expenditure generally reaches a climax upon the occasions when some Royal guest is received, or when, as in the case of the Temple Bar Memorial, an effort is made to bring the reigning family into personal contact with a Lord Mayor, so that a due recognition of civic merit may ensue. One example may suffice. A single day's entertainment to a Royal Prince recently cost £27,576. It included such items as—Refreshments, £5,098; Wine, £1,731; Upholstery, £4,534; Menu cards and banquet and ball tickets, £903; Badges for the Committee in the form of lockets, £300; Gloves, perfumery, and hair-brushes, £145;

&c., &c. Such an unaudited expenditure of public money carries its own condemnation.

The Court of Common Hall is a body without a parallel in existence. It is the assembly of the members of City Guilds who have taken out their Livery. It is not now called together—as formerly—for the transaction of the business of the City, but only for electoral purposes. It may, however, be regarded as the modern representative of the *immensa communitas* of the City under King Edward III. This body nominates the candidates for the Mayoralty, and elects the City Chamberlain or Treasurer, the Bridge-masters, City Auditors, &c. Court of Common Hall.

No reason remains for the preservation of municipal rights to the Liverymen of the City Guilds. These companies are integral parts of the Corporation, and whilst, on the one hand, important members of that Corporation owe their positions to the suffrages of the Livery, so, on the other hand, the companies are amenable to full control by the Corporation. The whole question of the position, work, income, and expenditure of the Livery companies is now *sub judice*, having been referred to an important commission appointed in 1880. Municipal rights of Liverymen.

In dealing with the establishment of a new Corporation, or the reconstruction and extension of the existing Corporation of the City, the practical course to be immediately adopted would seem to be to preserve to the Liverymen upon the register, at the time of the passing of the Act, the right of voting within the City for Common Councillors so long as they reside within twenty-five miles thereof, but to discontinue all electoral power as respects officers of the Corporation. The powers, jurisdiction, and control heretofore exercised or exercisable by the Corporation, or any of its courts, over the Livery companies, would remain until such time as the whole question of their constitution and functions should have been reported upon by the commission, and should be finally settled. Liverymen under new Corporation.

Down to the reign of King Edward III., London citizens were enrolled in the great hustings-court according to their inhabitancy within areas analogous to the Saxon territorial Origin of City Guilds.

guilds, and the united members of such areas formed the *communitas* or governing body of the City. During the later Norman and earlier Plantagenet kings London traders began to unite together for the benefit of their crafts, and formed mercantile guilds which ultimately controlled them. These later guilds governed and monopolised the separate trades, regulated prices, and assisted decayed members. The reign of Edward III. may be regarded as the period when the aggregation of gildated trades became more powerful than the collection of territorial guilds. Municipal rights passed into the hands of the trades, and some of such rights have remained there ever since. London being a community of traders, every prominent citizen of those days belonged to one or other of the trading companies; and, although in the course of centuries the connection of the Livery companies with trades has very largely ceased, yet some of the municipal rights have remained.

Former character of Guilds.

We have not space here to examine into the intensely interesting history of the formation, the growth, and the decadence of the Livery companies of London. In their early formation they were associations in which members of a given trade regulated its conduct throughout the capital and suburbs; where every man subscribed his quarterage to a common fund, had his voice in the ruling of the trade, was entitled to relief in case of necessity, and if he died in poverty was buried at the expense of the sorrowing brotherhood, at whose expense also the Company's chaplain said mass for the repose of his soul. In the present day the companies are generally divorced from the trade whose name they bear, and, whilst maintaining all the old forms of control, in practice enforce none.

Charters of the Guilds.

Nearly all the Livery companies exercise their rights under charters purchased from English sovereigns. These charters enabled the guilds on certain conditions to hold lands in mortmain, contrary to the statutes against it. The land so held has enormously increased in value, but the conditions precedent contained within the charters as to the management of trades, the admission of members, and other matters, are now rarely observed. Required by charter to teach the trade to all who chose to learn, and for "the greater good and common profit of the people," they have with a few exceptions long since disregarded these provisions. When every practiser of a trade was compelled to join a responsible guild, and every apprentice was bound to take up his freedom on pain of being sent to Newgate, a compact body of reputable tradesmen was found responsible for the credit of their craft, and, as the Wax Chandlers say in one of their petitions, "bore their charges towards the grandeur of this honourable City."

Down to a comparatively recent period both the City Corporation and the Crown possessed and exercised rights and control over the Livery companies. This control was actively asserted by every monarch, from Richard II. to William III., and their special privileges were only kept on foot by what may be termed subsidies to the Crown. Henry VIII. obtained £20,000 in 1545, for his Scotch war; Edward VI. received a similar sum; Queen Mary received £65,000 towards the cost of the French war; Queen Elizabeth extracted more than twice this sum from them; James I. incorporated fifteen new companies and granted new charters to old ones, all of which brought large sums to his treasury. At one assembly of the Common Hall, £100,000 was voted to King Charles I. Similarly large sums were paid under the Commonwealth, and afterwards to King Charles II. *Rights of Crown and City over Guilds.*

After the forfeiture of the City charters in 1684, the Livery companies of London voluntarily made submission to the king, and received new charters confirming the Royal control. But William III. was persuaded that this voluntary cession of the old charters was a tyrannous act of the late king, and anxious to conciliate the good will of an influential body of men, he willingly re-granted the old charters. When the report of the Guilds Commission is published, a new governing authority will be able to consider how far it may be concerned with these companies in the future. At present the City guilds have municipal functions, and are part of a municipal body; *New Charters in 1684.*

and possibly no inconsiderable proportion of an income of three-quarters of a million sterling per annum may be rightly available for municipal or trade purposes.

Charters of City of London. The Corporation of the City of London has no governing charter, and in that respect differs from most other ancient English Corporations. There are, however, something like 120 separate charters, which are supposed still to possess a certain amount of vital force, and which were granted to the City by various English sovereigns, commencing with William the Conqueror and ending with King George II. These charters may be regarded as the title-deeds of the Corporation, but they have never received authorised interpretation. Their language is often vague, archaic, and conflicting. They were granted in respect to a state of circumstances which has no modern parallel, and the extent of the privileges they were supposed to confer was generally measured by the extent of the consideration with which a powerful Corporation was able to tempt a needy monarch. Uncertainty as to the effect of some of these charters, and the still greater uncertainty as to how far subsequent charters repeal or affect former charters with which they conflict, has not, however, proved a matter of difficulty to the rulers of the City. Under the shelter of ancient prerogatives of undefinable extent, and of customs ripened by long prescription, or certified *ore tenus* by the mouth of the Recorder, the City have advanced claims of the most extensive character, and some which have been adverse to the rights of the surrounding population. In coming, however, to deal by an Act of Parliament with the question of an extended London government, we need not fear any suggestion on behalf of the existing Corporation that charters or customs cannot be superseded by an Act of Parliament. The doctrine that Royal charters cannot be abrogated except by other Royal charters was long held in the City of London; but the assertion of Sir Robert Peel at the time of the passing of the Municipal Corporations Act, 1835, that the Act "suspended all prerogatives of the Crown, and assumed for Parliament a right to supersede charters," undoubtedly expresses the true constitutional position of the matter.

In view of the facts as to the charters as they now exist, their undefinable character and extent, and their questionable validity, the best course to pursue with respect to them is formally to repeal them all, and, in the Act of Parliament constituting a new Corporation, to re-enact in clear terms such charters as are applicable to existing circumstances and likely to be of advantage to the community. There would be no injustice in claiming for the whole metropolis the benefit of these ancient charters whose advantages are now obtained for the City alone. Not merely would it be in exact accord with the principle and precedent of 1835, but an examination of the terms on which many of them were granted conclusively shows that they were intended for the benefit of the entire metropolis. The rights of holding lands in mortmain were rights granted to the entire capital, and much of the property held now by the Corporation of the City first came into their hands under charters given to the City when all the inhabitants were within the walls. *Method of dealing with Charters.*

If it were necessary to ascertain the exact effect and legal bearing of existing City charters, many questions of considerable nicety might arise. Down to the reign of King William III. it was the custom of City authorities to prostrate themselves before any newly-crowned monarch, and in the humblest language to solicit a re-grant of their charters. Since that time an entirely new doctrine has been advanced, to the effect that a re-grant by each successive sovereign, which was the preceding custom, was no longer necessary. In that complete settlement of the customary and written law of the City which was made in 1319, when King Edward II., after certain alterations and modifications, confirmed articles for perpetual observation in the City, the king in the exercise of his prerogative power limited and defined the privileges of the City, and confirmed them to be perpetually observed in the City and in the suburbs. These *Legal effect of Charters.*

c

suburbs to-day may rightly claim to enjoy all the privileges which have arisen under that charter, if its validity still remains. But as to the general question of the validity of the charters, we not only find that it was the custom of each sovereign to re-grant the charters of his predecessors, but that successive sovereigns claimed the right to modify the grants of their predecessors.

Confirmation of Charters.
The first charter of King Edward III. appears to lay down the principle upon which succeeding sovereigns acted. After enumerating and re-granting many City charters, the king granted that, "for the allowance of their charters, one writ should suffice in each reign." Nor does it appear that the writ was granted as a matter of course, for the very charter was "in consideration of the good services which the citizens had rendered to the king and his progenitors;" neither does it in this case appear to have been granted merely as a matter of pure prerogative, for we learn that it was by the assent of the prelates, earls, barons, and all the *communitas* of the realm then assembled in Parliament at Westminster. Many of the subsequent charters granted by succeeding kings were simply *inspeximus* charters, reciting and confirming preceding grants, but doing it with the assent of Parliament, and upon the petition of the citizens of London. Sometimes, as notably by King Henry VII., a large sum was demanded from the City before their charters were confirmed to them.

The *Quo warranto*: its effect.
Inspeximus charters were granted by King Charles I. and King Charles II., and the last of these, granted in 1663, has been regarded as the most valuable of the civic charters. It evidently contemplates the advantage of the whole capital city and suburbs. But according to a judgment of forfeiture in the well-known *Quo warranto* case in 35 Charles II., the charters of the City were forfeited. The alleged grounds of forfeiture included *inter alia* the establishment of tolls on markets rebuilt after the Fire, "whereby they scandalised the king's government and oppressed their fellow-subjects." The lan-

guage of the old charters, that the City's rights should continue, whether rightly used, or abused, or not used at all, does not seem to have stood them in much stead. Not long after the forfeiture of their charters, the City might be found on their knees at Windsor, confessing their faults and acknowledging the justice of their sentence ; but there was no re-grant of the City charters in this king's reign, nor any re-grant by King James II. Indeed, the latter monarch did not offer any until he learnt of the invitation to William of Orange.

The City exacted terms from William of Orange, and these terms are embodied in the statute 2 William and Mary, sess. 1, c. 8. The effect of this statute is to place the City in the enjoyment of its charters and rights as enjoyed before the *Quo warranto*. It amounts to a legislative repeal of the forfeiture, and the establishment of the *status quo ante*, but it neither affects, nor attempts to affect, the validity of the charters, or the necessity for their being re-granted in each succeeding reign. It has been suggested that a re-grant in each reign is to-day essential to their validity, and that they have now lapsed, but the establishment of such a position would be a difficult process, and the necessity for it is probably removed by the imminence of a complete reform. When the rights claimed by the City under its ancient charters have been contested they have always refused to disclose them, and by a standing order of the Common Council the officers of that body are precluded from showing the books or records to other than members of the Corporation without express license. The Commissioners of 1854 suggested the issue by the Crown of one comprehensive charter, incorporating all that was useful in existing charters and repealing the old ones. The customs of the City should also, in their opinion, be included in the new charter. In addition to Royal charters, the City constitution and rights are, of course, affected by Acts of the Legislature, but the Court of Aldermen and the Court of Common Council claim to have the power of modifying the constitution of the City by

City Charters at the Revolution.

ordinances and acts, and the customs and bye-laws of the Corporation are also alleged to have in certain cases the force of legislative enactments.

THE METROPOLITAN BOARD OF WORKS.

The Metropolitan Board of Works was constituted by the Metropolis Local Management Act, 1855. Before the passing of this Act the inhabited metropolitan area, outside the City of London, was in a state of chaos almost indescribable. The Corporation of the City had long since withdrawn from any effort to govern the suburbs around it, and the attempts of the later Tudor and earlier Stuart sovereigns to restrict the capital within the City walls were not repeated by any sovereigns of the House of Brunswick. Queen Elizabeth had prohibited the erection of more buildings, on the ground that so large a multitude would become ungovernable, and too great "to serve God and to obey Her Majesty." But the metropolis continued to grow, and beyond taking in some immediately outlying districts now known as Farringdon Without, Bishopsgate Without, and so on, the City exercised no control over it, and the outer districts were delivered over to such control as the parochial organisations could supply. The parishes were brought into intercommunication in the making of mortality returns, and subsequently for sewerage purposes, but otherwise large districts had separate local government, varying infinitely in character; and under many public, and more than 250 local, Acts of Parliament, at least 300 different bodies, with a membership of 10,000 persons, carried out what there was of local government in London. Boards of commissioners controlled streets and houses under Acts of Parliament of their own; surveyors and officers under building acts were appointed by magistrates and other persons over whom there was no popular control; and whilst some parts of the town lived under what Sir Benjamin Hall termed "the most extraordinary state of local management that ever existed in any country," there were other parts of the town absolutely without any local government whatever.

Into this chaos the Metropolis Local Management Act brought some sort of order. It constituted the Metropolitan Board as the central authority for drainage and some other purposes, and, proceeding upon parochial lines, provided for the establishment of what are now known as vestries and district boards over the rest of the metropolis. *[Metropolis Management Act, 1855.]*

The Metropolitan Board of Works is composed of 45 members in addition to a paid chairman. The members are elected for three years; one-third retiring every year. There is no approach to equality in the area, the population, or the rateable value of the districts by which the members are elected. If they were equally divided amongst the inhabitants of the metropolitan district, each member of the Board would have a constituency of some 80,000 people, representing a rateable value of more than half a million sterling. *[Constitution of Board.]*

The total area of the metropolis is 75,490 acres. The Holborn District Board and the Strand District Board each controls 167 acres, whilst Wandsworth District Board has 11,488. The population of Wandsworth is also several times larger than either of the smaller districts, but each of them sends one member to the Metropolitan Board. The discrepancies in the rateable value are still more remarkable. Whilst Woolwich, with a rateable value of £116,980, and St. George's-in-the-East, with a rateable value of £199,237, send one member each, Kensington, with a rateable value of £1,648,187, and Wandsworth, with a rateable value of £1,183,278, also send only one member each. There is, therefore, no sort of unity, equality, or system in the representation at the existing Board.

The Common Council of the City sends three members; the six larger vestries send two each; seventeen other vestries send one each; and the remaining thirteen are elected by district boards, a district board being an association of two or more vestries for administrative purposes. In the case of Plumstead and Lewisham (which are joined for electoral purposes) there are, for example, seven vestries, *[Representation at the Board.]*

and as the only direct popular election is to these vestries, it will be seen that many years might elapse before the seat of a member at the Board could be in any way affected by popular feeling.

<small>Sewerage Jurisdiction of Board.</small> The chief duty imposed upon the Metropolitan Board by the Metropolis Local Management Act, 1855, was the control of the system of main sewers throughout London. The authority previously exercised by the City Commissioners of Sewers and the Metropolitan Commissioners of Sewers was vested in them, and within three years from their constitution they undertook an extensive system of drainage which now carries the sewage from both sides of the river and a considerable part of the metropolitan area down to Barking and Crossness. At the time when the Metropolitan Board undertook the work, London drained directly into the river. The sewage system has now been so far completed that the metropolitan area is supposed to be free from sewage outlets. Down to the month of December, 1880, the Board had expended on main drainage and main sewers, £5,625,969. The Thames Conservancy Board consider that the river near the present sewage outfalls is being injured by banks of mud supposed to be formed by sewage deposit. The Board of Works have contested this proposition, and an enormously expensive arbitration, extending over five months, was the result. If there had been any unity of work between the two boards this would have been saved.

<small>Drainage System under new Corporation.</small> The arterial drainage system of London, extending over something like a hundred and twenty square miles of area, and accommodating more than four millions of people, must in any event remain in the hands of a central authority. The construction of the minor connecting drains which join the arterial drains to the houses is now made by the vestries and district boards. It is certainly desirable that the same authority which controls the main drainage should also undertake the making and inspection of the minor drainage, including drainage under

all new houses. There is reason to believe that many thousands of London houses simply drain into the sub-soil. This was found to be the case in six per cent. of the houses recently inspected by a sanitary association, and has been the cause of outbreaks of typhoid, even in large houses at the west end of London. Under a properly organised municipal system no house should be used as a dwelling until a certificate, or other evidence, had been obtained of its sanitary condition in this matter of drainage.

The Metropolitan Board of Works exercises a control over the embankment of the river, over the prevention of Thames floods, and over many of the bridges. The embankment of the river has been done under various acts of parliament at a total cost of £4,388,186. It is a work which reflects much credit upon those who have carried it out. The Board are also empowered, under the Thames River Prevention of Floods Act, 1879, to take measures for having the walls and banks of the river raised so as to prevent overflow in flood-time. They have prepared plans of forty-one miles of river frontage, and are proceeding to carry out the work in sections. *River Embankments and Floods Prevention.*

The Legislature have recently empowered the Board of Works to free the bridges over the Thames. Waterloo Bridge was purchased for £475,000, and Charing Cross foot-bridge for £98,540. These bridges were freed in 1878. Lambeth Bridge was purchased for £36,049, Vauxhall Bridge for £255,230, Chelsea Bridge for £75,000, Albert Suspension Bridge and Battersea Bridge together for £170,305. These bridges were freed in 1879. Wandsworth Bridge was purchased for £52,761, Putney Bridge for £58,000, Hammersmith Bridge for £112,500, and the bridge over Deptford Creek for £44,800. These bridges were freed in 1880. Blackfriars Bridge, Southwark Bridge, and London Bridge are the property of the Corporation of the City of London. Since acquiring the bridges for the public, the Metropolitan Board has expended considerable sums in putting them into repair; *Bridges.*

and they propose at great cost to rebuild Putney and Battersea bridges. Southwark Bridge was recently purchased and freed by the Corporation of London. The money was raised on the security of the Bridge House Estates. Blackfriars Bridge has been recently rebuilt with money borrowed on the same security. The rebuilding of one and the purchase of the other were carried out under the provisions of two Acts of Parliament passed in 1863 and 1867.

Bridges, Embankments, &c., under new Corporation.

There is no doubt that a central authority can well undertake the various functions in connection with the river Thames now discharged by the Metropolitan Board and the City Corporation. The bridges over the river can be usefully placed under a single control, and the income arising from the Bridge House Estates (upon which the building of London Bridge was originally charged) can be allocated as far as they will go to the maintenance of the bridges and the redemption of the debt upon them. The maintenance of the river embankments and the work yet to be done under the Floods Prevention Act may be also taken over without exciting needless friction. The central authority would then, through its representatives on the Thames Conservancy Board, control the traffic, and the locks, weirs, piers, and wharves on the river, together with the means for its purification; and would control directly its bridges, embankments, and walls. It would also control the supply of water from the river for such purposes of street-watering, sewer-flushing, or domestic use, as it thought fit. The conflict of jurisdictions would disappear, and the utmost possible purity of the stream be guaranteed, even though we could perhaps hardly expect to find a modern diplomatist following the precedent of the Spanish Ambassador to the Court of Elizabeth, and dilating on the "nobility of the river and the beauty of its hundreds of swans."

Street Improvements.

The Board has carried out large metropolitan street improvements under various acts of parliament passed for the purpose. The total expenditure for these improvements has amounted to £6,716,487. Under these acts Garrick Street, Southwark Street, Queen Victoria Street, and Northumberland Avenue may be quoted as illustrations of streets made; and the removal of Middle Row, Holborn, and the widening of Kensington High Street may be quoted as illustrations of the other class of street improvements. Some minor street improvements are also carried out by the vestries and district boards. It will scarcely be denied that the expenditure of such enormous sums of public money ought to be in the hands of a body of persons directly elected by, and responsible to, the ratepayers who provide the money.

In this matter of street improvements the principle has been accepted that the widening of an old thoroughfare, or the construction of a new one, is a matter sufficiently affecting the traffic and comfort of the whole town to be rightly chargeable on rates levied upon the whole area. This principle will not now be departed from. Such central authority ought also to have the control of all the minor street improvements now undertaken by vestries and district boards, and by the Corporation of the City of London. With a few exceptions in the case of new streets, a district in which street improvements now take place pays to the Metropolitan Board its full share of the cost, and there would therefore be no injustice in adding to the large Metropolitan Board street jurisdiction the smaller jurisdiction now exercised by the vestries. Under the existing system there is much danger of improvements being executed rather for local and personal reasons than for reasons of imminent public necessity. This danger has frequently proved a serious reality, but it would cease to be a danger in the hands of a central representative authority. *Street Improvements under new Corporation.*

Under various acts of parliament, the last of which was introduced by Mr. W. H. James, M.P., in 1881 the Metropolitan Board has been authorised to provide parks in the metropolis, and to acquire and control commons, gardens, and open spaces. *Parks, Commons, and Open Spaces.*

The cost of these has been defrayed out of a rate levied over the whole metropolis, and the Board now controls for the benefit of the public, Finsbury Park, Southwark Park, Victoria Park, Hampstead Heath, Blackheath, Leicester Square, Clapham Common, Wormwood Scrubs, and other commons and open spaces, covering a total area of 1,676 acres. The total cost of the acquirement of these properties has been under half a million sterling.

Parks, &c., under new Corporation. This jurisdiction must in any event be exercised by a central authority, and Londoners may look forward to the time when the other parks within the metropolitan area—Hyde Park, Regent's Park, St. James's Park, the Green Park, and Battersea Park, may be placed under the control of a London authority. At present, Londoners have no rights of ownership in these open spaces in their midst; and therefore the suggestion which is sometimes made, that they ought to be supported out of metropolitan rather than out of imperial funds, is absurd. So soon as terms of purchase and transfer are arranged, Londoners will no doubt be willing to undertake their charge. There is, in addition to the jurisdiction of the Metropolitan Board over parks and open spaces, an analogous jurisdiction exercised by the Corporation of the City of London, under which Epping Forest, Burnham Beeches, and West Ham Park have been secured for the benefit of the inhabitants. The control of these open spaces may very well pass into the hands of any new central authority.

Fire Brigade. In 1866 the Metropolitan Board took over the fire-engine establishment of the London fire insurance companies, and in the following year it took over the machinery and apparatus of the Society for the Protection of Life from Fire. Since these dates the Metropolitan Fire Brigade has, under the direction of the Board, discharged the duties of extinguishing fire and saving life. The staff of the London Fire Brigade is exceedingly small. For the protection of 3,800,000 people from fire, and for fire extinction, there are only employed 485 men all told. There are fifty-two fire-engine stations, five moveable stations, 117 fire-escape stations, four floating stations, 170 miles of telegraph, six fire-alarm circuits, three floating steam-engines, thirty-eight land steam-engines, 110 manual engines, and 135 fire-escapes. The City of Paris, with half the population of London, and covering far less than half its area, has a fire-brigade of 1,500 men, with fifty more fire-engines than there are in London. St. Petersburg, with a fifth of our population, has 1,149 firemen, Berlin has 1,000, Hamburg has 789, and Lyons, with less than one-tenth of our population, has a larger fire-brigade. The system which obtains in some American towns is still more elaborate. When the fire-brigade is in the hands of an intelligent municipal body, the system of fire-extinction will receive developments at present scarcely conceived of. As every one knows, the first half-hour of a fire is the most important, and therefore the means for its extinction should be brought to the spot with the utmost rapidity. But in London few means of communication with the nearest fire-office exist, and the communication is generally a matter of accident. The water has to be supplied from mains under the control of independent private water companies; no arrangement exists for obtaining the services of the turncock, and not one inhabitant in fifty has the least conception where he may be found.

A Select Committee in 1877 reported that the arrangements for the extinction of fire in London, "whereby the fire brigade is administered by the Metropolitan Board, where two separate police forces exist side by side, and the water supply is sectionally furnished by eight independent companies, were not such as to furnish adequate protection to life and property; and contrast unfavourably with provincial systems, where the fire brigade, water supply, and police are under a single authority." The police generally assist at the extinguishing of fire, but they have no control over either fire brigade or water company.

Inadequacy of present System.

American System.

If there were in London, as in many American cities, more numerous fixed points connected by telegraph with all the central fire and police stations, the waste of time would be reduced to a minimum; and when a central authority exists, controlling fire brigade and water supply, and also the civil force for the preservation of order, the serious fires in London will be very largely diminished. Neither is it too much to expect that water may be laid on at high pressure, and immediately available for the extinction of fire. Mainly composed of seafaring men, the London Fire Brigade is an admirably efficient body, but it is deficient in numbers, and, by reason of the multiplicity of independent authorities, it is deficient also in the power of making instantly available for its purposes all the public resources of the town.

Work of Fire Brigade.

The number of fires in London in 1880 was 1,871 but only 262, or nine per cent. of these, were serious fires. The number of lives lost was 33. In 44 cases serious damage arose from the absence or late supply of water through the fault of the water companies. The amount of water thrown by the Fire Brigade in 1880 was 21,072,739 gallons, of which about one-half was taken from the river. Towards the cost of the Fire Brigade the Treasury contributes £10,000 a year, and the fire insurance companies contribute a sum equivalent to £35 for each £1,000,000 insured. This latter contribution amounted in 1880 to £21,464. The remainder of the cost is defrayed by rate levied over the whole metropolis. The cost of the Brigade in 1880 was £88,980. The total expenditure on capital account since 1866 is £263,878.

Jurisdiction of M.B.W. under Building Acts.

It has often been contended by the opponents of a unified system of London government that a central authority would be unable to deal effectively with the details of municipal government, and that local interests would thus be neglected. The jurisdiction now exercised by the Metropolitan Board over buildings in the metropolis is an illustration of the possibility of the closest details of municipal government being directed from a single centre. Under several Acts of Parliament the Board now controls the height, cubical contents, frontage line, and other matters connected with buildings. It has a control over the foundations, so that houses can no longer be built on unhealthy rubbish which has artificially replaced valuable gravel. It has a control over the materials used and over the thickness of the walls. When the houses are built, the Board also controls the numbering and naming of the streets. It does not always do all this work intelligently, as the recent re-numbering of Oxford Street sufficiently shows, but the fact that, from a single centre, the regulation of the character of every building and the width of every new street and footpath in London is effectively controlled is a practical argument in the direction of the possibility of such an authority dealing with infinite detail.

The Board has, under the Metropolis Management Amendment Act, 1862, a veto over the closing of any street for repairs by a vestry or district board; and the control of a central authority ought to extend, as we shall presently show, to the making and maintenance of streets. Overhanging eaves, porticos, balconies, verandahs, chimney-shafts, wooden or concrete buildings are also required to have the sanction of the Board; and under the Metropolis Management Amendment Act, 1878, no new theatre or music-hall can be opened in the metropolis without a certificate of fitness from the Board. The supervision of dangerous structures was in 1869 transferred to the Board (except within the area of the City). Since that time the Board has dealt with more than 20,000 cases, and the buildings affected have been either repaired or removed. No less than 3,923 structures were so dealt with in the year 1880. *Further Building Jurisdiction.*

The control over all these matters is placed in the hands of surveyors acting under the architect of the Board, and for the purpose of carrying out the supervision London is divided into 67 districts. In 1879 more than 20,000 new buildings or *System of Building Control.*

alterations to buildings were carried out with the sanction of these surveyors. A new central authority would assume this jurisdiction, and with the assistance of the present surveyors of the Board, and the surveyors of the City, would carry it on as efficiently as at present.

Naming of Streets.
Alteration in the names and numbers of streets is carried out by the vestries under the authority of the Board. Under a central authority the representatives of any district would have a full opportunity of being heard, but the final decision would remain with the municipality. In 1880, 197 names for new streets were approved by the Board, 97 streets were re-named, 421 street names were abolished, and 10,173 houses were re-numbered. The whole of the building and street jurisdiction of the Board would be assumed by the new authority. If the Legislature originally thought fit to confer it on a single body when there were local bodies in existence able to undertake it, and if such central authority has done the work reasonably well, notwithstanding its inherent imperfection of constitution, it is not likely that it will now be suggested that the jurisdiction should be divided amongst a series of authorities.

Minor Jurisdictions of the Metropolitan Board.
In addition to the matters already considered, the Metropolitan Board of Works possesses jurisdiction and control over a number of subjects of less importance. Under an Act of 1874 the Board is empowered to regulate the carrying on within the metropolitan area of offensive trades. Most of the businesses included in this term have now been removed under the provisions of the Metropolitan Building Act of 1844, and with respect to those which remain, including soap-boilers, knackers, manure manufacturers, blood, tripe, and bone boilers, glue-makers and others, proceedings have been taken to render them as innocuous as possible. Licenses for slaughterhouses in London are obtained from justices at sessions, but the Board has a *locus standi* to oppose them, and the number has been reduced in the last seven years from 1,429 to 903.

Under the Explosives' Act of 1875 the Board regulates the manufacture, conveyance, storage, and sale of explosive substances in the metropolis. A good deal of effective work is done under the provisions of this Act. The Board also grants licenses in the metropolitan area outside the City for the keeping and sale of petroleum. More than two thousand such licenses are now current. Under the provisions of an order of the Privy Council, published under the powers conferred by section 34 of the Contagious Diseases (Animals) Act, 1878, the Board has for two years past exercised control over the trades of cowkeepers and milksellers, inspecting and regulating the lighting, ventilation, cleansing, drainage, and water-supply of dairies and cow-sheds. More than ten thousand inspections and reports upon cow-sheds, and more than twelve thousand inspections and reports upon dairies, were made under the supervision of the Board in 1880. There are at present in London about 1,000 licensed cow-sheds, and 7,000 dairies. Under the Contagious Diseases (Animals) Act, 1878, the Board is also the metropolitan local authority outside the City of London. Under this jurisdiction 378 animals affected with pleuro-pneumonia were slaughtered in the year 1880. The Board also dealt with 626 animals affected with foot and mouth disease, most of which however recovered. Ten outbreaks of typhoid fever of swine necessitated the slaughter of more than 100 of these animals. The veterinary inspectors of the Board in 1880 reported 1,806 cases of glanders and farcy in horses. In 1,758 of these cases the animals were slaughtered by the owners under notices served by the Board, and the majority of the remainder were either slaughtered by the Board's officers or died. The Board also insisted upon precautions in the case of the dairy and cattle shows held during the year. The sum of £7,403 was expended in carrying out these regulations as to diseased animals, most of the expenditure being in the payment of the compensations provided by the Act. In 1872 the Board was

Explosive substances.

Petroleum.

Dairy inspection, &c.

Diseases of Animals.

Infant Protection.

constituted the local authority for the inspection of houses where infants are received to be nursed for hire. During the year 1880 the exercise of this jurisdiction resulted in 341 inspections, and the number of registered houses is now twenty-three.

Minor Jurisdictions under new Corporation.

With respect to the subject of the various minor jurisdictions just considered, the Board is the local authority for the whole metropolitan area, with the exception of the square mile governed by the City of London. It has been the custom of the Corporation of the City, through its Remembrancer, to oppose the Metropolitan Board having any authority within the limits of the City. So far as independent exterior judgment can be formed, the Board has discharged its duties in the matter of these minor jurisdictions with credit to itself and with advantage to the community. They are all of them matters which may most usefully remain under the control of a central authority. Such central authority would take over the existing staff of inspectors and continue the work of the Board. There is no argument, except the fact of its existence, by which the continued separation for these purposes of a small area in the centre of London can be defended, and it is from every point of view desirable that the action of a central authority should be complete and uniform throughout the Metropolis.

Artisans' Dwellings.

Under the Artisans and Labourers Dwellings Act of 1875 the Board was appointed the local authority for the Metropolis outside the city of London. Under the provisions of the Act official representations have been made to the Board by the medical officers of health of different districts as to the condition of various areas unfit for human habitation. Upon these representations the Board has taken action in fourteen cases, and prepared schemes which have received the approval of Parliament. There is a considerable number of further representations, as to which no action has yet been taken. Great difficulties have arisen in the working of the Act, the procedure of which is found to be both dilatory and costly. In addition to this, the scale upon which compensation has been awarded in the case of houses that are removed, has been such as to render the working of the Act attended with great loss. Already the difference between the cost incurred and the monies received for cleared sites amounts to about three-quarters of a million sterling. The Board has, therefore, ceased to proceed with the carrying out of the Act, and the whole matter was referred in 1880 to a select committee of the House of Commons. The Acts contain no provision for the re-housing of the dispossessed poor, and their working has in this respect also been attended by much hardship.

<small>Accommodation for dispossessed Poor.</small>

The question of providing accommodation for the poor dispossessed in the carrying out of the provisions of an Act of Parliament, is considered in the Streets Improvement Act of 1877, and under the 33rd section of that Act the Board is required to ascertain that sufficient accommodation exists for dispossessed artizans when the number exceeds 15. The Board endeavoured, but unsuccessfully, to repeal this clause in 1881, alleging that it rendered the Act unworkable. The Board has in consequence abandoned some of its schemes for street improvements. This may be a loss for the time, but in the hands of a new Corporation, where the interests of the artizan poor would be adequately represented, the whole question will be likely to receive the fullest possible discussion.

<small>City Funds and the London Poor.</small>

The subject of the dwellings of the London poor is one of the utmost importance for the welfare of the people, partly because of the increased value of sites in the hands of private owners, and partly because of the deliberate action of the Corporation of the City in clearing vast areas covered by the dwellings of the poor, whereby the City is almost denuded of artizan population. Many of the City parishes contain no poor, and enormous funds left for the benefit of poor people residing within them are now otherwise appropriated. The funds left for local distribution were bequeathed at a period when the capital was contained within the walls, and every City parish had its adequate complement of rich and poor. In the hands of City guilds, City parishes, and other public bodies, these funds have increased in value with the increase of the value of City lands, until they now amount to several hundred thousand pounds sterling per annum. But the inhabitant poor of City parishes, who would be entitled to share in them, have been driven out to the east and to the west, to the north and to the south, and no longer receive any of the benefits intended for them. One of the first duties of a new Corporation will be to examine into this question, and to decide in what manner funds available for the education or assistance of the poor can be best utilised.

Metropolitan Board: Method of Work.

Discharging under 98 Acts of Parliament functions so enormous in their extent and so varied in their character, it may well be supposed that the 45 members of the Metropolitan Board of Works must devote the whole of their time to the public service, if they are to exercise any sort of intelligent control. During the year 1880 there were 363 meetings of the Board and of its committees. The work of the Board is carried out with the assistance of nine standing committees, of which one, the Bridges' Committee, was first constituted in 1880.

Municipal patriotism of Board.

The average attendance at the 43 Friday meetings of the Board has been 36. And if anything like the same proportion obtains with respect to the committees, each member must, on an average, have been present at the Board at least three days a week. The members come from every point of the metropolitan compass to discharge municipal functions which receive very little public recognition, which are entirely unremunerated, and the nature of which is unknown to the vast majority of Londoners. The debates at the Metropolitan Board are seldom fully reported; their action, and the reasons for it, in matters affecting the expenditure of millions of money, are rarely the object of public discussion, and never of effective criticism. A seat at the board is regarded as an estate for life, and only in rare instances does a member fail to receive the support of the vestry that originally elected him. Having regard to the conditions of its life, it may be doubted whether a similar instance of municipal patriotism can be found in the world.

After the Metropolitan Board was constituted in 1856, the rateable value of the Metropolis was £11,283,663. In the twenty-five years which have since elapsed it has risen to a sum of £27,847,875. The chief sources of the Board's income consist of loans, rates, and receipts from the coal and wine dues. There are also receipts from various sales of old materials, from interest on monies lent to other local bodies in London, and from rents and fees. The total liabilities of the Board at the end of the year 1880 amounted to £18,253,536. Of this sum £3,345,263 represented loans advanced to other local authorities in London, and £2,876,419 represented the estimated value of surplus land and property in the hands of the Board, leaving a net liability of rather more than twelve millions sterling. The amount of Metropolitan Consolidated Stock issued at the same date was £16,407,669. The loans to local authorities include the various Vestries, District Boards, Guardians, Burial Boards, Commissioners for Baths, and Managers for School and Sick Asylum Districts. It includes also £826,097 lent to the Metropolitan Asylums' Board, and £571,600 lent to the School Board for London.

The loans to various local authorities are made under the provisions of a number of Acts of Parliament passed during the last twelve years. The consent of the Treasury is given to each such loan, and also to all loans raised by the Board for its own purposes. An estimate is prepared each year by the Board, and incorporated in a money bill, which is afterwards introduced and carried by the Government of the day. Thus Parliament has the control over all loans raised in London. Except, however, so far as the preliminary examination by the Treasury may extend, this control is exercised in a very perfunctory manner, and the Board of Works' Money Bill generally passes without much criticism or notice. The borrowing of millions of money on the security of London rates is a matter therefore between the Treasury and the Board of Works, but a matter over which the ratepayers have no control, and of which they have no knowledge. Public criticism in London is unknown and impossible. Loans are granted to local authorities for purposes of capital expenditure upon street improvements, new buildings, purchase of land, and sewerage works. Large sums are also now borrowed for wood and granite paving. It is true that where money is borrowed for such temporary purposes as paving it is only lent for a short time—generally five or seven years—but the cost of this and other matters ought probably to be defrayed out of current expenditure.

Metropolitan Board: Capital Expenditure.

The capital expenditure of the Board, on its own works, in 1880 was £1,560,671, of which sum the larger portion was expended on street improvements and bridges. The Board has a power of contribution to minor street improvements carried out by Vestries, and by the Corporation of the City. In 1880, the amount so contributed was £52,998, being about one-half of the sum expended. Of other capital expenditure the Fire Brigade stations and plant absorbed £26,644. The loans advanced to local bodies amounted to £878,250, and the Board repaid of loans £436,533. Including these items, the total capital expenditure in 1880 was £2,955,620.

Current Expenditure.

The current expenditure of the Board amounted in 1880 to £885,641. Of this sum £623,319 was absorbed in the payment of interest on debt. This interest is payable on £16,407,669 Consolidated Stock at 3½ per cent., and £1,845,866 Main Drainage and other securities, including miscellaneous loans raised prior to the Loans Act of 1869, making together the gross liability of the Board £18,253,536. The borrowing of the Board is immensely in excess of its repayment, so that the debt of London is increasing rapidly.

From the formation of the Board to the end of the year

1880 the Board has applied in repayment of debt the sum of £8,023,539, of which sum about two-thirds was direct payment and the remainder accrued from conversion of the former debt into Metropolitan Stock. The credit of the Board in the Money Market has steadily increased. The price per £100 of Metropolitan Stock in November, 1869, was £94 14s. 10d. In 1880, it was £102 2s. 7d. So also the increase of rateable value has allowed of large increase of expenditure without much increase of rate; thus the rate levied in 1868 was £411,346, which involved a charge of 6·09d. in the £, whilst in 1881 a rate of £671,839 only involved a charge of 5·88d. in the £. Every penny of rate produces £116,000, and every additional £100,000 borrowed involves in the payment of interest and sinking fund a charge on the rates of ·045d. in the £. *[Repayment of Debt. Metropolitan Stock.]*

The remaining current expenditure of the Board, after payment of interest on loans, amounted in 1880 to £262,322. Of this sum the Fire Brigade absorbed £88,980. Sewerage and drainage expenses, £69,247; Embankments maintenance, £13,177; Bridges, £5,724. The establishment expenses amounted to £76,530, but only £43,468 of this is charged to current account. *[Net Current Expenditure.]*

The total income of the Board, capital and current, in 1880 was £3,157,988, and the total expenditure £3,841,262. The great discrepancy was supplied by a balance of more than £700,000 in hand at the beginning of the year. If we deduct from the expenditure the sum of £436,533 repayment of loans, we have an absolute expenditure in a single year by the Board of Works, or local authorities to whom it lends money (this latter being capital expenditure only) of £3,404,729. This is the revenue of a principality. It is raised from or on the security of the people of the Capital by only one of the Boards that claim to rule it, and that people have no direct representation on the Board, no voice in the expenditure, and no means of testing the right or wise appropriation of so enormous a fund. *[Total Income and Expenditure.]*

Vestries and District Boards.

The dividing limits of a parish are amongst the most enduring things known to our local life, and if a reasonably satisfactory means can be found of establishing a representative corporation without, in the first instance, interfering with them, it would tend to conciliate a most powerful opposition. These observations do not apply to the City of London, the circumstances of which are altogether exceptional, and where many of the 106 parishes have been altogether obliterated by the erection of large buildings, or swept away by modern improvements, until there often remains no parochial centre, nor even a church or vestry-room.

Divisions of London for Local Government.

The number of parishes in the metropolis outside the City is seventy-eight. Of these the twenty-three larger ones were adopted as self-governing centres under the Metropolis Local Management Act of 1855, for what may be termed minor municipal purposes. The remaining fifty-five were grouped together, in numbers varying from two to eight, as fifteen District Boards. There are thus thirty-eight authorities for minor municipal purposes. Where the government is by a District Board, the election is in the first instance to the vestry, and then the members of the District Board are elected by the vestries. Cases have recently occurred in which people defeated on the popular election for a vestry have been afterwards selected by the vestries as members of the District Boards. Vestrymen are elected for three years, one-third going out each year. Of the thirty-eight bodies thus ruling the outer metropolis, the number of members has been fixed according to the number of householders up to the limit of 120. This limit has been reached in the case of the larger parishes, and the present membership in the thirty-eight bodies aggregates nearly 3,000. The areas governed vary from 162 acres in St. James's, Westminster, to 11,488 in Wandsworth. The street mileage varies from eight miles in St. Martin's-in-the-Fields to more than 100 in Wandsworth.

The chief jurisdictions of the vestries and District Boards

are in a single group, and include paving, watering, cleansing, dusting, lighting, and minor drainage. With the exception of dusting, all these are concerned with the proper maintenance of the public highway. The removal of dust in London is a difficulty which has taxed these local bodies to the utmost. In some cases the vestries do the work themselves, and in others it is still delegated to contractors, who reap out of it a rich harvest of profit. Nearly everywhere there is an absence of regularity in the times of conducting the operation, although its total cost cannot be set down throughout London as much less than £150,000 a year. The greatest difficulty to be encountered is the method of disposal, as the hard core now possesses a far less commercial value than was formerly the case. The City authorities seem likely to adopt a method which has been proved successful in Leeds and elsewhere, of purification by fire, the whole material being destroyed in furnaces. This method of procedure seems to leave a profit on the operation. *(Vestry Jurisdictions. Dust Removal.)*

No municipal function is more purely mechanical than the removal of dust. It does not even require to be conducted under the eye of an inspector or surveyor. The cost of the operation at present varies enormously in the hands of different vestries. On the whole it is probably as well done in the City of London as in any metropolitan area. A Corporation governing the whole metropolis might, as matter of the purest mechanical arrangement, provide for the fortnightly emptying of every dust-bin at hours convenient to the inhabitants. Whether our system of dust-bins is better than American and foreign systems of household tubs placed on the causeway and emptied at night, is one of those questions which might well occupy the attention of a Public Works' Committee of a new Corporation, or—if the City system were extended as it now exists—of the new Commission of Sewers. *(Dust Removal under new Corporation.)*

The control which has been exercised by the vestries and District Boards over the paving, watering, cleansing, and lighting of London streets, has within twenty-five years com- *(Paving, Watering, Cleansing.)*

pletely changed the whole face of the metropolis, and there is at the present time no large American city which in the excellence of its roads can be for one moment compared with London. But the results have been acquired at very unequal cost, and are by no means of unvarying excellence. In answer to inquiries made a few years ago, it was found that on paving, watering, and cleansing different parishes varied in their expenditure from £364 per mile to £1,200 per mile, without sufficient difference of circumstance to justify it. The cost per mile of watering ranged from £11 per mile in Whitechapel, to £55 per mile in Lewisham; and the cartage of the water from £19 per mile in Mile End, to £70 per mile in St. Martin's-in-the-Fields. The cost of street lighting varied from £94 per mile in Bethnal Green, to £228 per mile in Marylebone. Amongst the thirty-eight vestries no less than eighteen different prices, varying from £3 10s. to £5 per lamp, were paid for the same quantity and quality of gas. In any unified system there would be a great saving in this expenditure. At present, in all these matters each vestry and District Board enters into its own contracts.

Defects of present Street Control.

The method of doing the work, the places in which particular kinds of pavement shall be laid, and the amount of light to be given in each street, are all of them matters of local discussion, and of necessity turn not infrequently upon local considerations. With such enormous variations in cost, there must of necessity be waste in some vestries, whilst there is parsimony in others; and it also may well happen that the parsimony is developed in the districts likely to suffer most from it. The proper expenditure upon municipal work will probably be found somewhere between the two limits.

Street Watering and Cleansing.

With respect to the paving, maintenance, watering, and cleansing of a street, it must be conceded that these ought in any case to be under uniform control. So far as watering is concerned, it is a purely mechanical operation, which might be directed by road inspectors or surveyors responsible to central authorities. An uniform and intelligible system would save a large amount of public money, even if the water were paid for as at present. But as a new water system would have as one of its essential points an unlimited supply of water for public purposes, the item of cost would be transferred to the water account, and its amount would depend on the cost at which the Corporation acquired a supply. In any event there would be a great saving. Street cleansing is also a mechanical matter, which ought to be systematically carried out. Some vestries do this work extremely well, and some scarcely do it at all. Like the inhabitants of Pittsburg, in Pennsylvania, they regard a heavy shower as the only proper agency for street cleansing. Sometimes very remarkable differences may be noticed in the same street when it passes through two or three local jurisdictions.

Street paving is a matter which in London requires much engineering and administrative skill. Some of the smaller vestries discuss it without this advantage. The consequences are patent to every citizen. The general result is fairly good, especially in the City of London and one or two of the West-end vestries, but the variations of price and of principle are almost infinite. Wood, asphalte, granite, and Macadam have each their proper place, but they must be used with a full understanding of the traffic and circumstances of each street. The large sums now being expended upon wood pavements in London require much more careful watching than they have yet received: and this pavement has been laid in some streets eminently unfit for it. Asphalte makes an excellent pavement where its conditions are understood. The City Commission of Sewers seem yet unable to understand that it ought to be washed perfectly clean every morning, so that it may give secure foothold. Granite is still the best street material for heavy and continuous traffic, especially where streets are not on a level, whilst for the ordinary broad suburban streets Macadam stands unapproached. But it

Street Paving at present and under new Corporation.

requires scientific laying, so that the whole may be welded together and a crown given to the road. The relaying of a street is a great disadvantage, and often a great loss to the inhabitants: it ought therefore to be done as rapidly as possible, and on what miners know as the three-shift system. Where there is a large number of streets to deal with, the municipal authority would have a large number of the most competent men in constant employ. The best engineering skill of the day would also be available for the initiation and superintendence of the work.

<small>Uniform Street Control.</small> The duration of the life of a well-made street varies according to the traffic upon it. But at present it rarely happens that the full value of a suburban street pavement is taken. Long before it is worn out the surface is broken up for the purpose of relaying or altering either pipes or drains, and constantly may be seen roads which have been paved with granite cubing on concrete, or Macadam compacted with great care by steam-rollers, torn up again with great toil and difficulty for some subterranean purpose. The waste of labour and money which has accrued from this source is enormous. It is true the disturbing authority is supposed to replace the street, but, as every engineer knows, it is practically impossible to do so. The crown of the road is broken, and the whole goes to pieces with great rapidity. Without mentioning the telegraph lines under the footpath, there are now four authorities with a right to tear up London streets, viz.:—The Metropolitan Board, for arterial drainage; the vestries, for minor drainage; the gas companies; and the water companies. Each of these authorities is practically irresponsible.

<small>Surface and Subterranean Street Control.</small> Efforts have been made to introduce a system of subways for pipes under streets, but such efforts have been unsuccessful, mainly through the non-concurrence of gas companies, the insecure joining of whose pipes might do less damage in earth than in a narrow passage. Surely it is not revolutionary to suggest that the whole municipal

action with reference to a street should be intelligent and uniform. Above and below there should be but one authority. No street should be relaid until it is ascertained that no cause exists underneath which will necessitate its disturbance until the surface is worn out. This unity of administration can best be attained by placing all the authorities in one hand. The making of a street is an engineering operation to be conducted on scientific principles, and with proper control could be well managed through London at an enormous saving of cost, and with a great increase of average efficiency. But such skill may be constantly wasted unless there is concurrent action between the surface authority and the subterranean authorities. From every point of view there would be an advantage in having them the same. In any event they must be the same as regards final control. The Commissioners of 1837 recommended that paving, sewage, and lighting should be under one authority in London.

The vestries have control over vaults, arches, and cellars under streets, and this may well be given to the same control as the authority controlling the Buildings' Acts and the streets. The same observations apply to the control given to vestries over the erection of hoardings, the sinking of wells, the fixing of pumps and drinking-fountains, and the cleansing of footpaths and crossings. Few vestries discharge their statutory duties in these matters. One or two have sunk wells and fixed pumps; a few assist in the supply of drinking-fountains, but this is usually left in the hands of a benevolent society whose chief expense is for water; whilst as to the cleansing of footpaths, vestries are careful in winter to evade their duty, and harry the householders under an old statute of King George III. *Minor Vestry Jurisdictions.*

Medical officers are appointed by the vestries to report on the sanitary condition of the parishes. It is upon the report of these officers that the Board of Works proceeds under the Artisans Dwellings Act. They present reports to the vestries *Medical Officers.*

on all matters within their province. Some reports are exhaustive and valuable; others are poor and valueless. Some vestries pay their officers highly, others merely give them a retaining fee. In this matter unity of administration and procedure would be of untold benefit. Where the sanitation of the town is worst, the medical inspection is also the feeblest. A committee controlling matters of public health would soon reduce all to one system and to complete order. The same observations apply in a still more forcible degree to the Inspectors of Nuisances appointed by vestries. The theory of a witness before Mr. Aryton's Local Taxation Committee, that "each vestryman is an unpaid sanitary inspector," is, unfortunately, an unpractical dream.

Rates.

The Vestries and District Boards are the agencies for the collection of public rates. They collect the Metropolitan Consolidated rate, for the purposes of the Board of Works; a General rate, for the purposes of the School Board and for their own general purposes; a Vestry Sewers' rate; and a Lighting rate. The Poors' rate is sometimes also collected by the Vestry; but the practice varies, according to the provisions of many local acts. The Poors' rate includes the expenses of the Guardians; County and Lunatic charges; Police rate, and costs of preparing registers, jury lists, &c. An extended Corporation may well consider the whole question of London rating, but at the outset there would be no difficulty in the Corporation settling the proportion of rate to be paid by each London parish, and then, by order under its common seal, requiring overseers to levy it, as many of the Vestries and district Boards now require the overseers of the parishes within them to levy their rate. The whole rate-collecting machinery would thus be adapted to the new system without much change.

Local Taxation.

A new council would also, no doubt, examine into the very difficult question of the incidence of local taxation. On all hands the present system is admitted to be unfair, but it is by no means easy to devise a satisfactory substitute. In many American towns the Gordian knot has been cut by requiring every citizen to make a declaration of the total amount of his possessions, after paying his just debts. These amounts are then aggregated, and the rate levied upon the whole. As the amounts are published, it is supposed that the number of people who represent their possessions as less than they are, is equalled by those who are willing to pay a rate on a higher representation than the fact. In London, a man with £20,000 in Consols may live at ease in a house at a rental of £100 a year, whilst a tradesman who, after paying his just debts, has only £2,000 capital, must, for the purpose of his business, rent a shop at £100 a year. These two men pay the same municipal rates. In Boston the capitalist would pay ten times as much as the tradesman. Probably no such inquisitorial system would be accepted here, but the whole subject is one deserving the closest attention of an intelligent public body. London rates press very hardly upon tradesmen, and a School Board rate of 3s. 6d. per head of our population works more hardships here than a School rate averaging £1 per head in Boston.

The Vestries have powers under the Baths and Washhouses Act; but they have only been put in force in a few places and by a few Vestries. These institutions ought to be provided all over the Metropolis, as St. Martin's-in-the-Fields and St. James', Westminster, have shown us they can be made self-supporting. The boon conferred by such institutions on the poorer classes of the people is incalculable. *Baths and Washhouses.*

Only a few of the Vestries have established mortuaries. A recent grave scandal in the parish of St. Marylebone has drawn attention to the condition in this respect of that great parish. Ambulances and disinfecting-chambers are also wanting to many Vestries. The enforcement of the Adulteration Act is very uneven. There are other powers, as to bakehouses inspection; powers under the Sanitary Acts; powers as to lodging-houses and other matters, all of which would readily *Mortuaries, Adulteration Acts, &c.*

fall into their place in an unified central system. The varied benefits contemplated by numerous Acts of Parliament would no longer be lost to the districts most requiring them, and the health and convenience of the people would be attended to with a completeness and economy which is not now even approached.

<small>Tramway Jurisdiction now and under new Corporation.</small>

Under the Tramways Act of 1870, the consent of the Vestries must be obtained to their construction, and also the consent of the Metropolitan Board. When these consents are obtained, promoters may proceed by way of provisional orders made by the Board of Trade, and afterwards confirmed by Parliament, or by way of a bill in Parliament simply. If a responsible central authority were created for the whole of London, the necessity for the controlling action of the Board of Trade, or for going through the process of a private bill in the House of Commons, need no longer exist. It might be necessary to have formal Parliamentary sanction, but even this could be safely dispensed with when there was a certainty that the whole bearings of the question would be adequately considered by a representative body. Their control would also extend to road locomotives, and to an examination of all railway schemes affecting the metropolis. The report of the Corporation on these would probably affect materially the decision of Parliament upon them, and enormously lighten its labours. At present, if a dozen railway or tramway schemes are presented to Parliament, proposing to tear up our streets and demolish our houses on lines of route selected by promoters, the people of London are practically unprotected. No Parliamentary Committee can adequately judge of the requirements of London in these respects, but a representative Council with local assistance would do so.

<small>Ecclesiastical Jurisdiction.</small>

There only remains a series of jurisdictions incident to Vestries as ecclesiastical bodies, rather than as Municipal organisations. These functions may in the first instance be well left in the hands of the ecclesiastical Vestry until such time as a new Corporation may have time to consider their merits. There are income and expenditure affecting churches and parochial charities which belong to this class.

These varied functions are not such as tempt the ambition of the average Londoner. Vestry elections were expected by the framers of the Act of 1855 to be severely contested. Occasionally this is so, where some special agitation has been promoted, but frequently the number of persons electing is less than the number to be elected, and frequently there is no contest at all. As a rule, not one in a hundred of the inhabitants of the vestry area have any knowledge whatever as to the date of an election, or as to its results, or as to the names of the vestrymen, or their work, or anything about them.

Vestry Elections.

An Act of Parliament passed in 1852, providing for the discontinuance—with certain exceptions—of burials within the metropolitan area, made provision for the establishment of Burial Boards in London, and also for the establishment of cemeteries. The Act has been repeatedly extended, and further powers given. There is a considerable number of Burial Boards within the metropolitan area. The Commissioners of Sewers of the City of London are the Burial Board for the City, and have under their control an enormous cemetery at Ilford. The Burial Boards outside the City have been generally appointed under the provisions of Sect. 10 of the Act of 1852, providing for the convening of Vestry meetings to determine whether the Act shall app'y to the parish. Outside the City there are 27 Burial Boards in London. Their total income in the year ending Lady Day, 1880, was £43,817, of which the greater part was supplied by burial fees, but a deficiency of £6,955 was charged on the poors' rate. The expenditure was £45,155. The loan liability was £129,660. If the present City Corporation were accepted as the initial basis of a new Municipality, the committee which succeeded to the functions of the Commission of Sewers would assume the control now exercised by the various Burial Boards

Burial Boards.

of London. The Secretary of State possesses a power as to making regulations as to interments. These regulations are of the most complete character, but when the cemetery system of London comes to be considered by an intelligent representative body, a question may well be raised whether the duty of a Municipal government to its citizens is confined to providing well-drained and accessible cemeteries, and whether it does not also extend to the provision of facilities for rapid and economical burial. This duty has been undertaken in Paris and some other cities, whereby the cost of performing this last service to humanity has been very largely lessened.

Vestries and District Boards: Income and Expenditure.

The Metropolitan Local Management receipts in the year 1879–80 amounted to £2,549,837. Of this sum there was raised by rates £1,796,661, and by loan £753,176. The expenditure was divided as follows:—Street control, including paving, cleansing, and watering, £1,229,808; lighting, &c. £247,820; sewerage, £136,335; repayment of loans, &c., £329,826; salaries and collectors' poundage, £126,601; miscellaneous, £240,919. The outstanding loans amounted to £2,416,549.

Loans.

Audit of Vestry Accounts.

The Vestry accounts are supposed to be audited, but the auditors are elected by Vestries, and are not necessarily qualified persons. Their functions are supposed to be discharged by a verification of vouchers for expenditure. Technically, they have under the Act of 1855 a power of surcharge, but, curiously enough, there is no power of enforcing it. No surcharge has ever therefore been sustained, and the expenditure of funds levied by rates is not always limited to public purposes. One important London district in 1880 appointed no auditor at all.

Vestry Reports.

The Vestries are required to prepare yearly reports of their proceedings. Some prepare books as voluminous and complete as a Boston School report, others are content with a few pages. There is no single matter dealt with in the same way, and many are not mentioned at all. Comparison of work is therefore impossible. Some Vestries also publish, either at the back of the rate-warrants or elsewhere, a statement of the addresses of parish officers, and the situation of mortuaries, washhouses, fire-escape stations, and so on. Other Vestries do nothing of the kind, and the average Londoner has no conception of what Municipal conveniences exist, or where they may be found.

A provision is contained in the Metropolis Local Management Act of 1855 whereby the benefits of that Act may be extended to parishes adjoining the Metropolis with not less than 750 inhabitants rated to the poor. This may be done by Order in Council. A similar power might be granted in a new incorporating act, so that when the Corporation had settled the most useful boundary it would not be needful to come to Parliament with a special bill. But the question is one of much importance. Not merely are there large adjoining districts, like West Ham, with an immense urban population, but there are also within the present Board of Works area, districts in Lewisham, Plumstead, and elsewhere, which are essentially rural, and the retention of which within the Metropolitan limit is at least deserving of the most careful consideration.

Metropolitan Boundary.

In addition to the Corporation and City of London the Metropolis contains what are inaccurately termed "the Corporation and City of Westminster." The area of this City is supposed to be co-terminous with that of the Borough of Westminster, but the term "City" is as inapplicable to it as the term Corporation is inapplicable to the body of gentlemen who exercise authority within it. There is no Town Corporate with a Bishop, but there is a Cathedral Church. This Church of St. Peter, Westminster, traces back its history to the days of King Edward the Confessor, who having, when a refugee in Normandy, vowed a pilgrimage to Rome if God would free him from his distress, was afterwards, on ascending the English throne, relieved from this vow by the Pope on condition of his

"Corporation" of Westminster

E

expending a sum equivalent to the cost of his pilgrimage in raising a shrine to St. Peter. A monastery on the banks of the Thames, which had suffered much from the ravages of the Danes, was rebuilt, and endowed by charter with absolute jurisdiction over surrounding land. For more than 500 years the area around the Church of St. Peter's at Westminster was under the direct control of the Abbots and Monks of St. Peter, and, at the suppression of the monasteries, this was found to be by far the richest foundation in the kingdom.

"City" of Westminster.

Henry VIII. changed the monastery into a College of Secular Canons under the government of a Dean, but in 1541 he again changed it into a Bishopric with a Bishop, Dean, and twelve Prebendaries, and for a diocese the whole County of Middlesex except Fulham. Since that time the term "City" has been applied to Westminster, and the name was not lost when the Bishopric was dissolved by King Edward VI. After having been placed once again under a Dean by King Edward, and restored to the monks by Queen Mary, Westminster was, by letters patent from Queen Elizabeth, erected into a College under the government of a Dean, Canons, and Prebendaries, and all the privileges and customs of the old monastery extended to it. Confirmatory letters patent were granted by King James I., with full manorial and other rights over the whole City of Westminster except the precinct of the Savoy.

Former Divisions and Jurisdictions.

These powers, which are of various kinds, are now never exercised; and a division of the city made in 1585 into twelve wards, each of them to be under the government of a Burgess appointed by the ecclesiastical rulers, practically no longer exists. These Burgesses were entitled to exercise the same authority as Aldermen of the City of London, and power was given to the Dean and Burgesses together to make orders for the good government of the inhabitants. An Act of King George II., passed in 1756, makes further provision with respect to the government of the city. Many other Acts of Parliament were subsequently passed, affecting cleaning, paving, lighting, and the preventing of nuisances in the city, but the only municipal work now undertaken by the Dean and Burgesses of Westminster appears to be the appointment of an Inspector of Weights and Measures.

There are sixteen Burgesses and sixteen Assistant Burgesses, appointed annually in Easter week, according to old custom. The officers of the "Corporation" consist of the Dean of Westminster, a High Steward, a Deputy High Steward, a Town Clerk, a High Constable, a Crier and Mace-bearer, a Summoning Officer, a High Bailiff, and a Deputy Bailiff. We have not space to enter into an examination of the functions discharged by these officers. There is, moreover, a "Clerk of the Markets," but there are no markets; and there is a "Searcher of the Sanctuary," but Westminster has long ceased to be a refuge for the "abandoned miscreants" who, as Maitland tells us, formerly lived there in impunity and open defiance of justice under the charter of sanctuary of King Edward the Confessor. Members and Officers of "Corporation."

The income of the "Corporation" consists of the sum of £500 a year, paid out of the Civil List, and the fines levied by the Court of Burgesses. Thus there are not many festivities; and the silver snuff-box, the property of the Corporation, is in more frequent requisition than the loving cup presented by Maurice Pickering, centuries ago. The whole institution is moribund; and when uniform regulations are made for the execution throughout London of the law as to weights and measures, and also for the performance of the formal duties now discharged by the Bailiff of Westminster, the "Corporation" may be extinguished, and its functions absorbed, to the advantage of everybody concerned. The £500, paid yearly out of the Civil List, is not under Parliamentary control, the amount of such list having been settled for the present reign at the time of the accession of Her Majesty. The income may be utilised for the present in compensating such of the officers of the Corporation as cannot be usefully enlisted in the service of a new municipal authority. Income of "Corporation" of Westminster.

TOWER OF LONDON.

In addition to the City of London there is another imperium within the metropolitan area, and that is, the government of the Tower. As a Royal palace and fortress, this is under the control of a Field Marshal as "Constable of the Tower," assisted by a Deputy Lieutenant, a full official staff, and a large body of magistrates. The Courts of Kings Bench and Common Pleas were formerly held here, greatly to the advantage of the City. The Sovereign frequently lived here, down to a period within 200 years, and the liberties and franchises of the Tower have been repeatedly the subject of examination in consequence of the conflicting claims and privileges of the City. They appear to have been finally set out and confirmed in letters patent granted by King James II.

Present Jurisdiction.

The area of the Liberties of the Tower has been curtailed by the Police Act, and under the Central Criminal Court Act and County Court Acts its criminal and civil jurisdiction would appear to have been to a large extent taken away. If it be still regarded as a Royal fortress, its shadowy jurisdiction may be permitted to remain if confined within the limits of the moat. But perhaps the time may come when, ceasing to be either a fortress or "a place of arms," it might safely be placed under the control of the same Council which directed the management of other places of public resort in London.

COUNTY JURISDICTIONS IN LONDON.

All the schemes of London government reform introduced in recent years have provided for the constitution of the metropolis as a county to itself. At present it is situated in the counties of Middlesex, Kent, and Surrey, and contains within it the county of the City of London. In many respects the government of these counties remains similar to the government of other English counties, and with Lords Lieutenant, High Sheriffs, Justices of the Peace, and Clerks of the Peace, they take no cognizance of the enormous metropolitan population within them. The High Sheriff of Middlesex, who may be regarded as the principal civil representative of the Crown in the county, is elected at the same time as the Sheriff of the

City by the Liverymen of the City Guilds, meeting in Common Hall.

If London is constituted a county of itself it will be necessary to decide whether the privilege exercised by the Crown in other counties shall be extended to London, or whether the right of appointing its own sheriff shall be preserved. The Sheriffwick of Middlesex was first granted to the citizens of London by a charter of King Henry the First. Perhaps a satisfactory solution of the question might be found if the Crown were to resume the Sheriffwick of such part of the county of Middlesex as lies outside the metropolitan area, and to grant to the Corporation the Sheriffwick of such parts of the counties of Surrey and Kent as lie within such area. The new Corporation might then appoint two sheriffs, one with jurisdiction on the north side of the river, and one with jurisdiction on the south side. *Sheriffwicks.*

The special Acts which have been passed providing for the holding of two sessions of the Peace in Middlesex every month may be adapted for the metropolitan area, and the Surrey Sessions be confined to the county outside the metropolis. The various matters of county control would be assumed by a new Municipal authority, and an adjustment made of the proportionate rights of the district in existing lunatic asylums and other property. The necessity for separate rating in respect to county matters would be removed. With the magistracy of aldermen gone, with stipendiary magistrates exercising jurisdiction over the whole area, and with the licensing authority changed, there would scarcely remain any useful purpose to be served in London by the perpetuation of an unpaid body of Justices of the Peace. *County Jurisdictions under new Corporation.*

Under the Elementary Education Act, 1870, London was made the subject of special treatment. The whole metropolis was united into one school district, with ten divisions for electoral purposes. The desirability of establishing ten separate School Boards in London was the subject of much anxious thought *School Board for London.*

on the part of the promoters of the Education Act, but the balance of advantage pointed to one Board for the whole of the metropolis. The decision has been attended with the happiest possible results. It was found that a public body to which the Legislature had assigned almost plenary power in educational matters was an object of ambition to a class of men who had never before volunteered for municipal work. Men occupying prominent positions in the educational world, or who had formed through experience or study pronounced opinions upon educational questions, were found willing to devote several hours a week from their busy lives to the work of laying the foundations of an educational system for the metropolis. And nobly has that work been performed. During the first nine years of its life the Board settled finally the character of the public education which should be given, the limits to which it should extend, and the principles which ought rightly to control the government of a vast educational system in London. That work is now done, and large numbers of children are receiving in London Board Schools a substantial and practical educational training.

Class of Members.
With their work accomplished, the founders of the system have in some cases withdrawn themselves from the Board, and their places have been taken by others, who are not perhaps all of the same type. But the machinery is now perfected and at work, and little remains but to adapt it to the extended conditions of the town, and watch over its smooth running. Even if it were true that there were depreciation in the type of members of the School Board, as is sometimes alleged, this would not therefore furnish any ground for the assertion sometimes made that the necessary tendency of elected municipal bodies is to depreciate in character.

Number of Children and School provision.
Ten years ago it was estimated that the proportion of children between 3 and 13 years of age in England and Wales was 23·58 per 100 persons, but that in London the proportion was only 20·86. If this proportion be applied

to the recent census of the district over which the London School Board exercises its sway, it will be found that the number of children of school age in the metropolis is 799,437. It has been found that about one-seventh of the children in London belong to the classes which are able to pay 9d. a week or upwards. Deducting this one-seventh, there remain in London 685,240 children with respect to whom the Board have the responsibility of seeing that they receive efficient elementary education. In certain cases also the Board is now entitled to require attendance at school of a considerable number of the 70,000 children between 13 and 14 years of age. It is needful, however, to make many deductions on account of the necessary absence of children from various causes, so that the total number of school places which ought to be absolutely provided is somewhat more than 600,000. The present provision in efficient voluntary schools in London is 266,071, and in Board schools 236,024, making a total of 502,095. There is, therefore, still a great deficiency of school accommodation; but as schools for nearly 100,000 children are already in various stages of progress, it is probable that before very long this great educational agency will be abreast of the necessities of the time. The effect of the system in London has been to weed out the inefficient class of voluntary schools, so that those now remaining are well able to hold their own and supply a distinct public want, as may be judged from the fact that only two were transferred to the London School Board in 1880–81.

The buildings of the Board are erected with great care and solidity, and the convenience and completeness of their arrangements are the result of the fullest consideration and adaptation of means to an end. The general regulations as to subjects taught are of course controlled by the new Code issued by the Education Department at Whitehall, but the excellence of the teaching is indicated by the fact that the percentage of passes in reading, writing, and

Buildings, Character of Teaching, &c.

arithmetic is nearly 6 per cent. higher in London than in the provinces. The actual average of education is also rising fast; in 1878 1 in 5 of the children reached the Fourth Standard, in 1881 the number had risen to 1 in 3.

Cost.

The net expenditure on school maintenance per child was £1 12s. 8d. in 1874, and £1 12s. 9d. in 1881; but the gross cost has been recently some 25s. per head higher in consequence of the enormous number of new schools; this cost will, however, rapidly lessen as the school accommodation approaches completion. The distribution of the teaching staff is arranged on the principle of allowing to a head teacher or a pupil teacher 30 children, and to an assistant adult teacher 60 children. The average salary of an adult male teacher is £144, being £23 more than the average of provincial schools the average of an adult female teacher, £108, being an average of £36 more than in the provinces.

School Attendance, &c.

At present the educational system of London suffers in comparison with many others, especially in America, from the absence of efficient normal schools and training colleges. The School Board controls, through a Bye-laws Committee, the attendance at both Board and voluntary schools throughout the metropolis, but the percentage of average attendance has never been higher than 80·4—the attendance in 1880. This compares well with other towns, such as Birmingham with 73, or Bristol with 65, but is not a satisfactory final proportion. The working of the compulsory law is found to be attended with greater harshness since the Summary Jurisdiction Act of 1879 changed the penalty from fine and imprisonment to fine and distress. The School Board has been the means of rescuing large numbers of children from vagabond life. It has three Industrial Schools under its own management, and—reckoning places elsewhere—has 3,150 children in schools of this class. Of these children more than 90 per cent. turn out well. The conjoint working of the London educational system and of the Industrial Schools Acts is rapidly reducing juvenile crime in the metropolis. In 1870 the number of juvenile commitments was 10,000, and in 1880 very little more than half that number. Truant boys, and boys over whom parents have no control, are sent for short periods to a truant school under the control of the Board. The discipline at the school is severe, but judging from the fact that the average attendance at school of children after leaving it is 92 per cent., it would seem to be effectual.

The School Board for London is a remarkable illustration of the possibility of a central authority controlling the details of a great metropolitan work. Whilst the School Board lays down the general principles upon which particular questions are to be decided, the actual detail work is carried out by officers working under the direction of committees. The members of each of the ten divisions meet also as a separate committee to consider the requirements of the division. They control for the division the action of the Superintendent and Visitors —officers whose function is that of enforcing attendance of children at school. They also exercise a general control over the appointment of Managers, and part of the action of the divisional committees. It is usual to place three or four schools in the same neighbourhood under the control of a body of ladies and gentlemen known as School Managers, who visit the schools, watch the conduct of the teachers, examine the condition of the buildings, advise upon the fee to be charged in new schools, decide upon applications for remission of fees, examine and select candidates for the post of teacher, and otherwise act in the management of the schools. As a rule their action is confirmed when necessary, and teachers or assistants selected by them are generally appointed by the Board. School Managers are appointed by the School Board on the nomination of a majority of the members of the Board for the particular division in which the group of schools to which they are appointed is situated. The service which these ladies and

Details of School Board Work and Management.

gentlemen have rendered throughout London has materially assisted the School Board system, and they would probably remain, in any future system. They very usefully supplement the local knowledge and control of the divisional members.

Income and Expenditure of School Board.

The capital expenditure of the Board for the year ending March 31, 1881, was £566,375. Of this sum £395,420 was expended in the purchase of land and erection of buildings, and £170,955 in payment of interest and the repayment of principal on loans. The current expenditure of the Board for the same period was £668,981. This sum included £53,116 for administration, £39,021 contributions to industrial schools, £10,498 for sundry fittings and furniture, and £566,346 for school maintenance. This latter sum was on an average attendance for the year of 198,395 children. Amongst the expenses of school maintenance were:—Salaries of teachers, £435,053; furniture and cleaning, £32,633; rent and rates, £31,626; books, apparatus, and stationery, £28,905; repairs, £14,134; fuel and light, £12,150; sundries, £11,843, making a gross cost per child of £2 17s. 1d. Towards this cost in the same period the Board received from sources other than loans or rates the sum of £241,394, being at the rate of £1 4s. 4d. per child, and making the net cost £1 12s. 9d. The receipts included £152,288 for Government grant, £81,639 for school fees, and £7,465 from sundry sources. The Government grant averaged 15s. 4d. per child, and the school fees 8s. 3d. per child. The total capital and current expenditure of the year was, therefore, £1,235,356. Towards this sum there were actually received of Parliamentary grants £163,469, and from loans towards the capital expenditure £395,420, making together £558,889, and leaving a net expenditure of £676,469. Towards this there was received from rates during the year £629,623, being at the rate of somewhat over 6d. in the pound.

Loan Liability of School Board.

The liabilities of the Board at the end of the year were £4,349,013. Of this sum £3,446,767 was borrowed from the Public Works Loan Commissioners, and £571,600 from the Metropolitan Board of Works. The balance represents other liabilities of the Board. The total expenditure for purchase of land up to the end of March, 1880, was £1,579,447, for building of schools £2,287,189, and for school furniture £113,649. The total amount of loans repaid is £157,151.

There are few institutions in London that could be so readily absorbed into a central municipal system as the School Board. As a matter of convenience and for the purpose of avoiding needless friction, it might be wise to omit any provisions for this purpose from a new incorporating Act, and the matter might be relegated to the consideration of the new Corporation, who might, if they thought fit, afterwards elaborate a scheme upon the matter; but with the London educational system settled and solidified, its working might be very safely entrusted to an Education Committee of the new Council. There would in such event be upon the Council many members of former School Boards, and thus the continuity of its life would be maintained. A committee of 40 members might contain representatives from every part of London, and might very well have referred to it the whole question of the provision of public libraries. The Union and District Schools, and also the Industrial Schools, would be under its control. The control of the City of London School and the Freeman's Orphan School would be transferred to it, and probably effective action would be taken with regard to the Charterhouse School, Christ's Hospital, and other educational institutions. *[School Board under Municipal System.]*

A representative Central Council in London controlling the education of our people, the maintenance of our poor, and the provision of libraries and recreation grounds for the public, would be likely to take useful action in the direction of the utilisation of the vast endowments left for the education and assistance of the poor. Some years ago the London School Board, after investigating into the facts as to some of these *[Utilization of Endowments.]*

endowments, the administration of which is now in the hands of City parochial authorities and of City Livery Companies, made a claim in the interests of London elementary and suggested industrial education upon such funds of about £160,000 a year. This claim only represented a small portion of the funds which may be ultimately found available for public purposes in London. But the London School Board, although representing by direct election nearly four millions of people, has not been able to enforce its claim, and those who are now in possession of these funds pay no regard to the suggestions and requests of the Board.

<small>Endowments under new Corporation.</small>

When a Central London Council comes to take this question in hand, a practical result may be confidently anticipated. The right to re-appropriate these endowments for educational purposes was claimed by the School Board on many grounds, and especially in accordance with the principle of the 30th section of the Endowed Schools Act, 1869, which provides for the appropriation to educational purposes of endowments for the giving of doles in money or kind, marriage portions, redemption of prisoners and captives, relief of prisoners for debt, loans, apprenticeship fees, and other purposes which have failed or become insignificant in character while the income has increased abnormally. The circumstances of parochial and other endowments in the City of London bring them directly within the provisions of this statute. Where the property of the endowment is in City land or houses it has enormously increased in value, but the objects of it have in some cases disappeared altogether. Where the gifts to the poor are limited to City areas, there are now no poor within such areas; where money is left to apprentice boys, there are now no boys to apprentice; and it is a common principle of equity that the charitable objects originally intended should be effected by as near a re-appropriation as may be. At present the trustees of these endowments cannot find outlets for them; and the City parish authorities alone, pay more than £10,000 a year out of charity funds towards lessening the poor rate paid by householders in wealthy City parishes.

The whole question is one of much intricacy, but the facts are becoming more fully known, and when a representative body has completely ascertained them it will be able to suggest such a reappropriation as shall be in accordance with precedent, and, whilst duly regarding the intention of founders, may also be just to the poorer citizens of the capital for whose benefit the funds were mainly intended.

POOR LAW ADMINISTRATION IN LONDON.

In dealing with the existing forms of government in London it is not necessary to say very much with respect to the administration of the Poor Law, except so far as such administration presents features peculiar to the metropolis. For Poor Law purposes London has been dealt with specially since the passing of the Houseless Poor Acts of 1864–65, and the completer measure known as the Metropolitan Poor Act, 1867. For Poor Law purposes London is divided into five districts, and thirty unions or parishes. The variations in population and rateable value between these thirty areas, each under its separate Board or Guardians, is very considerable. About two-thirds of the Guardians are elected by voting papers, each householder having one vote for each £50 rateable value of his house up to £250. He may thus have six votes if his rent is over £250, and if he is also owner of such a house he would have six more votes. These votes cannot, however, be cumulated. The number of elected Guardians is supplemented by nominated Guardians, a body which includes all the Justices of the Peace.

Metropolitan Common Poor Fund.

Since 1867 a Metropolitan Common Poor Fund has been available for the maintenance of lunatic and insane poor; of persons suffering from contagious and infectious diseases; for the payment of salaries, of compensations, of registration fees, of vaccination fees, and other matters; the relief of casual paupers; and a considerable portion of the cost of the maintenance of indoor poor. This fund is levied on the rateable value of the whole metropolis, and covers 42·3 per cent. of the cost of poor relief in London. The amount paid to this fund in 1880 was £769,648. Under this system the richer districts of London contributed to the poorer the sum of £171,591.

Poor Relief: Indoor and Outdoor Relief.
The total amount paid for Metropolitan Poor Relief in 1880 was £1,817,972, being about 10s. per head of the population, and equivalent to a rate of 1s. 5¾d. in the £ (the lowest rate for ten years, with the exception of 1877, which was the same). There was expended in 1880 on indoor relief (which included inmates of workhouses, infirmaries, separate and district schools, asylums for imbeciles, fever and small pox hospitals, certified schools, institutions for deaf, dumb, and blind, convalescent homes and training ships) £513,775, and for outdoor relief £198,422, total £712,197. The outdoor relief is now less than one-half of what it was ten years ago.

Statistics of London Pauperism.
The number of paupers in London in 1880 was, indoor 48,251, outdoor 50,665, total 98,916, or 27 per 1,000 on estimated population. In 1871 the proportion was 47 per 1,000. In December, 1880, there were in twenty infirmaries and sick asylums, 7,944 persons; in four Metropolitan District asylums, 4,726; in seven asylum hospitals, 836; in forty workhouses, 25,362; and in eighteen pauper schools and one training ship, 11,026. Forty-seven dispensaries have been established for the benefit of the outdoor poor, at which more than one million prescriptions were made up in 1880.

Metropolitan Asylums Board.
The Metropolitan Poor Act, 1867, provided for the combination of unions and parishes into asylum districts, and the erection, support, and maintenance of asylums for the relief of the sick, insane, or infirm metropolitan poor. A body, since known as "The Metropolitan Asylums Board," was incorporated as a Board to manage asylums provided in pursuance of this Act, and the whole metropolis was combined into a district, termed the Metropolitan Asylums District. The cost of managing the asylums is defrayed rateably over the whole metropolis, but the expenses of inmates are chargeable to the

unions or parishes whence they come. Of the sixty members of the Board fifteen are nominated by the Local Government Board, and forty-five elected by the unions and parishes. The Board have purchased sites and built hospitals in various parts of London; but that part of their jurisdiction which extends to the poor suffering from infectious disease has been the subject of much adverse action on the part of inhabitants of the districts where their hospitals were placed. After much litigation, it has been decided that the Act of 1867 does not confer upon the Board any right to maintain a hospital if it should prove to be a nuisance to the district in which it is situated. There is much evidence to show that small-pox hospitals become nests of contagion to surrounding districts, and this part of the work of the Board has been attended with extreme difficulty. Some of its hospitals have been closed, and it is not improbable that the system of aggregating large numbers of patients under the roof of one single hospital will receive reconsideration.

The Board expended in 1880 £373,377. Of this £91,790 was expended in the maintenance and funeral of patients. The other items of expenditure are concerned with the maintenance of the hospitals under the charge of the Board, and range from a sum of £32,243 for the salaries of officers, down to the interesting item of £861 for tobacco and snuff. The local expenditure was divided amongst the hospitals under charge of the Board as follows:—Caterham Asylum, £52,525; Leavesden Asylum, £46,341; Darenth Schools and Asylum, £30,606; The Exmouth Training Ship and Infirmary, £22,177; Deptford Hospital, £21,875; Homerton Fever Hospital, £15,644; Homerton Small-Pox Hospital, £10,384; Stockwell Fever Hospital, £9,702; Fulham Hospital, £7,723; Stockwell Small-Pox Hospital, £6,566. The central office expenses were £5,594. The amount of loans repaid, £18,493. The total outstanding liabilities of the Metropolitan Asylums Board on the 26th day of March, 1881, was £873,649.

Income and Expenditure of Metropolitan Asylums Board.

Central Control of Poor Law system.

The whole working of the Poor Law system in London is under the direct control of the Local Government Board, but the great necessity of the situation is the establishment of a central municipal authority. Such authority would be able to reduce to a system the varying practices of different Boards as to the method of dealing with applications for medical aid, for poor law relief, and other matters. Such an authority would also control the workhouse system of the metropolis, classify completely the inmates, and distribute the cost of infirmaries and sick asylums over the whole metropolis. It would also probably extend the Common Poor Fund system to the whole poor law expenditure.

Ultimate transfer of Boards of Guardians to new Corporation.

Owing to the controlling hand of the Local Government Board, the action of the Boards of Guardians in London is not so widely varying as that of the Vestries and District Boards. But if the whole work of poor relief could be directed from an administrative centre, there would be a great saving of cost and a great gain in efficiency. It is not likely that in the first instance any proposal would be made to transfer the poor law system to any central municipal Council, but before such council had been long constituted the advantages and the necessity of such a transfer would become apparent, and means taken to effect it. The performance of the various duties now discharged by boards of guardians could be discharged by local committees, and there can be but little doubt that the transfer of such functions to such committees would endow the latter with sufficient importance to make them objects of legitimate ambition to good men in each district, and especially to the better class of those who have hitherto been discharging the work of Poor Law Guardians. The advantage of having a directly elected central council, controlling expenditure upon workhouses, dispensaries, infirmaries, union and district schools, and other matters, would be shown in an enormous saving of the cost of supply, and in a unification and systematisation of procedure which would be of great advantage.

It is possible that in some form the control of the Local Government Board might be usefully continued for a time, but that might well remain for decision after a full examination of the situation, and an estimate of the capacity of the new council. The position of the Metropolitan Asylums Board and its very peculiar jurisdiction would necessitate the consideration by the new Corporation at a very early period of the whole question of poor relief, and there can be no doubt that the consolidation of system and the direct control of all expenditure which would prove advantageous in all other matters of municipal government, would also be found beneficial here. The Royal and other Hospitals of the Metropolis would come under an even more direct control than that which would exist through members of the Council being appointed governors. *[margin: Final Control by new Corporation.]*

With the classification of the poor in separate workhouses; the establishment of casual wards; a settlement of the character of the labour test; the extent and nature of gratuitous medical relief; the settlement of the principles of out-door and in-door relief; of the method of dealing with the houseless poor, of the sick and infirm poor, and the poor suffering from contagious disease; with the care and classification of the lunatic and insane poor; the control of public vaccination; and the control and adaptation of existing charities and charitable foundations, a Committee of the new Corporation, composed of representatives from various metropolitan districts, might occupy itself and the Corporation for a lengthened period. But the result would be in all respects for the public advantage. *[margin: Result of Central Control.]*

The union of parish clerks, for the preparation of tables of mortality, first made in 1562 in the various parishes of the metropolis, and continued down to the present century, was a purely voluntary union. For a long time the parishes acted together for this purpose, and London came to be regarded as the area of the 148 parishes included in the bills of mortality. The union of parishes for this purpose, commencing with the defection of St. George's, Hanover Square, in 1823, was gra- *[margin: Registration Returns.]*

F

dually broken up. The mortality returns previously supplied by the parish clerks have now been collected under the provisions of the various Registration Acts. The metropolis of the Registrar-General is nearly, but not exactly, coterminous with the jurisdiction of the Metropolitan Board of Works. For the purposes of Registration London is divided into five main divisions and twenty-eight registration districts. The number of registrars and assistant registrars in each district varies according to the population. The number of officials, exclusive of those at the central office, is between two and three hundred. The cost of the central office is defrayed by the imperial Treasury. The cost of the local registrars is defrayed out of the London Poor-rate, and their appointment is in the hands of the various Boards of Guardians.

METRO-POLITAN POLICE. The police force of London is under two separate and independent jurisdictions. The management of the police force controlling the area of the City is in the hands of the Common Council of the City. The management of the metropolitan police, controlling a large area known as the Metropolitan Police District, is appointed by the Home Secretary. The inhabitants of the metropolis outside the City of London are therefore deprived of that control over the forces of public order which provincial corporations to a large extent possess. They are at the same time required to defray by rate the same proportion of its cost.

Necessity of Uniform Police System. Whatever may be the proper hands into which the control of the London police should be given, there can be no question that the present duplicate system must be abolished. Some years ago Sir Richard Mayne pointed out that "the existence of a detached police force in the heart of the metropolis is at variance with the principles upon which police are established in every other town in the kingdom." The Commissioners of 1837, condemning the duplicate system of police as it then existed, say, "We can see no middle course for the establishment of an efficient police through the metropolis between placing the whole under a metropolitan municipality and entrusting the whole to commissioners or other similar officers under the immediate control of your Majesty's Government." A vigorous attempt was made in 1839, by Lord Melbourne's administration, to include the City police in the metropolitan system. With respect to the City police at that time, a committee of the House of Commons had reported that "if a scheme should be contrived for increasing vice and crime, nothing could be better calculated than the system of police in the City of London." "In my whole experience," said Lord Brougham, "I have never seen so strong a censure, so unsparing a condemnation, passed upon any system whatever; above all, upon any system venerable from its antiquity, most of all, upon any system touching nearly upon the attributes of justice!" With their own system condemned by every committee of the House of Commons during the preceding forty-five years; condemned by Lord John Russell, Sir Robert Peel, and every leading man in and out of Parliament, the City nevertheless succeeded—by means which Lord Brougham denounced in scathing language, a few years later—in defeating the attempt of the Government to unify the metropolitan police force.

We have already mentioned the ignominious failure of Sir George Grey, in 1863, in his attempt to amalgamate the two police forces. It was the last of the many recommendations of the Commissioners of 1854 which he endeavoured to carry into law. So it remains that at present the governing statutes of the metropolitan and City police forces are the 2 & 3 Vic., c. 47, and 2 & 3 Vic., c. 94. The Treasury do not contribute to the City Police Force as they do to the Metropolitan Force, so that the City now pays a large sum which would be recouped by the Treasury if the system were unified. It is not necessary here to examine the special functions of this civil force, or the manner in which they have been discharged. Some of those functions are undoubtedly

Present Control.

such as should be in the hands of a municipal authority. The inspection of cabs, omnibuses, public carriages and horses, the regulation of street traffic, the abatement of the smoke nuisance, the inspection of lodging houses, and matters of that kind, clearly come within this category.

Principle applicable to Control of Police.

Lord John Russell laid down the true principle of police control when he said that it ought to be in the hands of those who are responsible for the peace of the town. In a certain sense, therefore, the object contended for by the City, notwithstanding the unprincipled manner in which it was pursued, was a constitutionally just one. With the control of our police in the hands of Government, the responsibility which citizens should bear in the maintenance of the peace of their town—a responsibility which was fully accepted in all our ancient systems of local government in England—is seriously lessened, and one of the most powerful securities for public liberty removed. In London, at the present moment, is a disciplined army of 10,000 men, trained to military movements, unaccountable to either Parliament or the people, but under the absolute control of the Home Secretary of the day. Such a state of things may be not untruly described as a usurpation of popular rights.

Police under new Corporation.

A new central authority, responsible for the preservation of public order, ought to have the direction of the civil force through which such order is to be maintained. A provision for the transfer of the metropolitan police force from the Home Office to the new Corporation might be included in its constituting Act. But there are many difficulties and jealousies in the way; and, indeed, there is an influential class of persons who are anxious to place the whole police force of the country under the direct control ot the Government. The introduction of such a provision in a constituting Act would therefore excite much opposition from people who might otherwise be willing to accept the principle as a measure of London reform. It would, perhaps, therefore, be wiser to let the matter stand over. The City police would become an appanage of any municipality which absorbed or extended the City, and the proposition in the Municipality Bill of 1880, that the outside force should be transferred, after a scheme to be settled by the Home Secretary, might indicate a safe solution as to the rest.

The present metropolitan police district extends 15 miles from Charing Cross. The new police district might be coterminous with the new municipality, whenever its boundaries are settled, and the rest of the present police district be absorbed in the various counties to which it may belong. *Metropolitan Police District.*

The City police in 1880 cost £100,601, of which the amount expended in wages was £70,698. It is now a very efficient body. *City Police: Cost.*

The total expenditure on the Metropolitan Police Force for the year ending March 31, 1881, was £1,176,074. The income from rate warrants issued to the various places within the Metropolitan Police District was £555,843; from Imperial funds, £451,181; from amounts received from various persons and authorities for the special service of the police, £127,179; on account of carriage licensing, £27,655; and some minor receipts. The expenditure included a sum of £118,005 contributed towards the Police Superannuation Fund. This sum forms the main income of a fund which now amounts to more than £150,000. *Metropolitan Police: Cost.*

The metropolitan police force consisted at the end of the year 1880 of 25 superintendents, 603 inspectors, 922 sergeants, and 9,393 constables, making a total of 10,943. There was an increase of 245 during the year, a number which could scarcely be considered excessive, having regard to the fact that in 1880 70 miles of fresh streets and 24,945 houses were added within the district. The duties of the force are, upon the whole, efficiently performed. The metropolitan police discharge many duties in addition to the primary one of the protection of the town. No less than 10,860 children and 3,338 adults were reported as lost or missing; 29,297 stray dogs were seized by *Strength and Work of Police force.*

the police; and proceedings were taken against 899 persons for furious riding or driving. The lost property department of the police received 16,849 articles, of an estimated value of £22,000; these articles were returned to their owners when found. The police, under the Common Lodging House Acts, exercised inspection over 1,439 non-registered lodging-houses and over 1,235 registered houses, accommodating 26,071 lodgers. The control exercised by the police over public locomotion involved the issue of 12,261 licences to hackney and stage carriages, and 20,446 to hackney and stage drivers.

LONDON CABS.

The first Act affecting hackney carriages in London was passed in 1662, and from that time down to the year 1869, the Imperial Parliament has regulated by statute this branch of public locomotion in London. In the reign of Charles the Second the hackney carriage license of £5 was applied towards the cost of paving and sewerage. Under William and Mary an increased duty was applied towards liquidating the cost of the French war, and a long series of subsequent Acts, now repealed, made various provisions for the regulation of hackney carriages, and for the appointment of commissioners to deal with offences. It is, however, to be noted, that down to 1831 all such offences were dealt with by civil process. Between 1831 and 1869 eight Acts of Parliament on the subject have been passed, and they now embody the laws by which London hackney carriages are controlled. There does not exist on the Statute Book any more unpractical and arbitrary body of laws.

Hardships of existing Law.

The placing of London hackney carriage control in the hands of the police, and the reference to a police tribunal of even the most trivial offences, is a matter as to which a useful body of public servants have just cause of complaint. The wearing of a defaced badge, the carrying of too many passengers, the plying for hire elsewhere than on a standing, the taking—even under special agreement—of an excess fare, or even the absence of a check-string, are made matters punishable by fine and imprisonment. But whilst in these cases a cabman can be at once compelled to go to the nearest police station, a hirer may defraud the driver of his fare, or even damage his cab, without the driver having any remedy, except by summons against some person unknown. The fares are arbitrarily fixed for Highgate Hill as for the Strand; for day and for night; for fine weather and for deep snow. Any agreement to pay more than the fare is invalid, but any agreement to pay less than the fare is good. Such laws could only be made by an overtaxed Legislature unfamiliar with the circumstances of the trade.

It is necessary, at the earliest possible moment, to relieve the Legislature of all control over London locomotion, and to give it to a representative body, before which all interests affected may be properly heard. A civil tribunal may well deal with all civil offences, and the functions of the police in the matter be confined to cases of intoxication, furious driving, injury to person or property, assault, and such other matters as come rightly within their province. In other towns the control of all public locomotion is, to a large extent, in the hands of a representative authority. It is right and just that it should be so in London. Such body would make regulations for all public locomotion, and would also be the licensing authority, and thus, through themselves or through commissioners appointed for the purpose, would possess as much control over civil offences, and over the whole trade, as the public interest could demand. *Control of Locomotion under new Corporation*

The control of the two rivers of the metropolis, the Thames and the Lea, is in the hands of two bodies, known respectively as the Thames Conservancy Board and the Lea Conservancy Board. The Corporation of London exercised the right of conservancy of the Thames from Staines Bridge to Yantlet Creek in Kent from a very early period down to the year 1857. The claim of the City rested upon ancient grants of the Crown and on long-continued usage, and the power was exer- *Thames Conservancy Board.*

cised by what was known as the Thames Navigation Committee of the Common Council. In 1857 (by the 20 & 21 Vic. c. 147) the Thames Conservancy Board was constituted, and the exclusive jurisdiction of the City abolished. The constituting Act provided for the appointment of twelve conservators, some of whom were by virtue of their official positions better acquainted with the work likely to devolve upon such a Board than were an accidental committee of the City Corporation. The bed, soil, and shores of the river are vested in the Conservators, and they have extensive powers of control over the river traffic. In 1864 the number of Conservators was increased to 18, and finally in 1866, by the Thames Navigation Act, the number was increased to 23. Prior to the passing of this latter Act the jurisdiction of the Conservancy Board had been coterminous with the former jurisdiction of the Corporation— that is to say, from Staines Bridge to Yantlet Creek in Kent; and the control of the Thames and Isis from Staines to Cricklade in Wiltshire was vested in a separate body of Conservators possessing varied and incongruous qualifications.

Constitution of Board.

The Thames Navigation Act, 1866, for the first time placed the control of the whole river, from Cricklade to the Medway, under one Board. This Board now consists of the Lord Mayor of London *ex-officio*, two Aldermen of London, four members of the Common Council of the City, the Deputy-Master of the Trinity House, two members nominated by the Lord High Admiral, one by the Privy Council, one by the Trinity House, two by registered ship-owners, two by owners of lighters and steam tugs on the river, one by owners of river steamers, one by dock owners and wharfingers, one by the Board of Trade, and four by the persons who were qualified to be Commissioners under the Act of 1795, which was the governing Act of the Conservators of the Higher Navigation before their absorption in 1866.

Nature of River Control.

The control exercised by the Conservators over the river has been of great benefit. Locks have been re-built; old mooring stations have been repaired, and new ones constructed; weirs have been repaired; the navigation has been improved, and strenuous efforts have been made to exclude from the river the refuse of paper mills and the sewage product of the towns upon its banks. Great as has been the success attending many of these measures, it is not possible to anticipate any complete results, so far as purification is concerned. The enormous increase of the riparian population, now several hundred thousand in number, and the increasing use of chemical manures, render absolute purity in our great metropolitan river unattainable. When the sewage of all riparian towns is excluded, we may expect to have a stream which will be inoffensive even in the greatest droughts of summer, and which may well supply the metropolis with water for public purposes and for baser domestic uses, but no process of purification can make it fit for the permanent potable water supply of the capital.

The accounts of the Boards amalgamated in 1866 are kept separate, and the funds of each made available for the portion of the river to which they apply. The total net receipts of the Lower Navigation Fund for the year 1880 were £80,550. This sum included £36,327 for tonnage dues, £8,921 for tolls, £8,029 for pier dues, £2,800 from water and canal companies, and £6,099 for rents for accommodation. The expenditure for the same period was £88,636, and was mainly incurred in connection with the maintenance of the navigation, dredging, repairing locks, weirs, and piers, inspection of explosives, removal of wrecks and obstructions, and so forth. The capital account of the funds shows a sum of £102,400, borrowed on the security of the tolls. *Income and Expenditure: Lower Navigation.*

The accounts of the Upper Navigation show receipts £27,691 16s. 1d., and expenditure £21,198 12s. 11d. The chief items of receipts are contributions from the water companies, £12,050. Considerable expenditure on capital account is still going on in this part of the river. *Income and Expenditure: Upper Navigation.*

LEA CONSERVANCY BOARD.

The Lea Conservancy Board was constituted by a private Act of Parliament in the year 1868. Prior to that date the control of the river had been in the hands of trustees appointed in accordance with various Lea Navigation Acts. The number of conservators under the Act of 1868 is thirteen. Five of these are appointed by persons interested in the district through which the river runs; two by the New River Water Company; two by the East London Water Company; one by the Corporation of the City of London; one by the Metropolitan Board of Works; one by barge owners, and one by riparian towns. This Board controls the river Lea and its tributaries from its source in county Bedford down to the limit of the Thames Conservancy jurisdiction, 200 feet below Barking Bridge. Its powers are analogous to those possessed by the Thames Conservancy Board, and include the control of the navigation, the traffic and all matters affecting the purity of the river. As to this latter point, however, the same observations apply as have already been made as to the larger river. Notwithstanding the efforts of both bodies of conservators, the water of both rivers is, as is hereafter shown, slowly but surely deteriorating, and, however useful for other purposes, they cannot any longer be made properly available for the supply of drinking water.

Lea Conservancy; Income and Expenditure.

The receipts of the Lea Conservancy Board for the year ending March 31, 1881, were £24,040, of which £15,468 were from water rentals, and £3,557 from tolls. The payments were £23,660. Of this sum there was interest on loans £7,764, and sinking fund, £1,500. The cost of works and repairs was £8,245, and £1,000 was paid as remuneration to the Conservators. The remaining charges were chiefly for establishment purposes. The debt of the Board on April 1, 1881, amounted to £184,367, secured by debentures.

Rivers Conservancy under new Corporation.

The Commissioners of 1854 expressed the opinion that the management of the Thames navigation was not in harmony with the ordinary municipal duties of the Common Council, and in coming to consider how far the control of our metropolitan rivers ought to be in an elected municipal body, the cogency of this opinion must be admitted to be as strong in relation to such a body as it was thirty years ago in relation to the Common Council. It would be a hazardous experiment to absorb these two Conservancy Boards into a new municipality, trusting to the chance of members being elected to the municipality possessed of adequate technical knowledge to control the work of the present Boards through a Conservancy Committee. A safer course to pursue would be to leave the Boards in the first instance untouched, save that the seven members of the Thames Conservancy Board now sent from the City Corporation should be nominated by the new municipal authority, and that the six members of the Lea Conservancy Board, now nominated by the water companies, Corporation of London, and the Metropolitan Board of Works, should be replaced by a similar number to be nominated by the new municipal authority. The future relations of the two Conservancy Boards to the Municipal Council might then very well be left for future discussion and arrangement. The Council would, through its representatives, obtain a substantial initial influence at the councils of the Conservancy Boards, and if, upon mature consideration guided by experience, it were found desirable to strengthen such influence, there is no doubt that Parliament would readily hearken to any application by the Council in that direction.

The water supply of London is now provided by eight private companies. The "New River" Company takes its supplies from springs in Hertfordshire and from the River Lea; the "East London" Company is chiefly supplied from the River Lea; the "Kent" Company is supplied from wells sunk in the chalk; the other five companies, the "Chelsea," "West Middlesex," "Grand Junction," "Lambeth," and "Southwark and Vauxhall" are all supplied from the River Thames. According to the sixth report of the Rivers Pollution Commissioners, published in 1874, the water of both the *[London Water Supply. Sources of Supply. Nature of Supply.]*

Thames and the Lea was in a very much polluted condition above the intake of the water companies. These commissioners therefore recommend that both rivers should, as early as possible, be abandoned as sources of potable water. Dr. Frankland, the analyst to the Local Government Board, has also constantly in recent years reported the presence in the London water supply of much sewage contamination, and in the Local Government Board Report for 1880 he states that it was only during three months of that year that the water sent out by the companies drawing from river sources was even in some measure fit to drink.

Amount of Supply.

The average amount of water delivered by the companies in 1880 was 142,000,000 gallons per day, being an increase of nearly 8,000,000 gallons on 1879. Of this amount more than 71,000,000 gallons were, we are informed, sometimes "grossly polluted by sewage matters." More than 61,000,000 gallons were "occasionally so polluted," and less than 9,000,000 gallons were uniformly of excellent quality for drinking. These figures are an eloquent condemnation of the policy of purchasing at an exorbitant rate so imperfect a supply. *It is noted that the impurity is increasing, and was greater, both proportionately and actually, in 1880 than during any year since the analyses began in 1868.* Dr. Frankland also states that the water of both the rivers is becoming year by year less suitable for domestic use.

Unsuitability of Supply.

This condition of things is most serious, as it is admitted on all hands that the supply of water is essentially a municipal function. It is an article of primary necessity, and upon its pure and sufficient supply depends in a large degree the health of the town. Under various Acts of Parliament, ending with the Metropolis Water Act, 1871, the water companies are subject to public control, and they have expended large sums of money in completing systems of filtration, but from the nature of the river water with which they had to deal the result has been always unsatisfactory, and—as the Rivers Pollution Commissioners say—no process has yet been devised of cleansing water once contaminated with sewage so as to make it fit for drinking. If therefore the citizens of Greater London purchased the existing water supply, one of the first duties of the purchasing authority would be to initiate a fresh supply for potable purposes.

In 1878 the Metropolitan Board of Works proposed a scheme for a supply of 16,000,000 gallons a day of pure water from the chalk strata under London, to be laid on at high pressure in new pipes under the footpaths, so as to be available for drinking and fire brigade purposes. Engineers gave their sanction to the scheme, and estimated the cost of carrying it out at less than six millions sterling. During the session of the Select Committee on Water Supply, in 1880, two eminent engineers estimated the cost of a supply of river water from the Thames above Teddington Lock, laid on in unlimited quantity for public purposes and the lower domestic uses, at £6,000,000 sterling, so that if the ground were unoccupied London might have a duplicate and final supply for £12,000,000 sterling. The present supply amounts to about thirty-five gallons a head per diem. In a non-manufacturing town this points to great waste, and experience has shown that with a system of constant supply fifteen gallons per head is sufficient. If this be so, we are informed on high authority, that more than sixty million gallons a day of the purest water could be readily obtained from the strata round London. *Cost of New Supply.*

In March, 1880, the then Home Secretary introduced a measure for the purchase of the existing companies. The London consumers were not consulted in any way in the matter, nor was there any public body in existence of sufficient importance to be taken into the Government counsels upon it, as the pretensions of the Metropolitan Board put forward two years before had been definitively rejected by the Legislature. The basis of purchase embodied in the Water Trust Bill of *Water Trust Bill of 1880.*

1880 was that each water shareholder should receive an amount of 3½ per cent. stock, sufficient to produce him the same income which he derived from his water shares, with prospective increase in respect of expected increase of value in the succeeding twelve years. Thus an absolute security was to be given for one of speculative commercial value. The value of the immediate annuities in 3½ per cent. stock at par was £22,098,700, and the present value of the deferred annuities was £6,851,300, making the value of the stock under the agreements £28,950,000. If the deferred annuities had been capitalised at 3½ per cent., the total amount would be £29,734,281. To this must be added preferential and debenture capital £3,061,500, and mortgage and bond debt £223,055, making a total for the purchase of the companies of £33,018,836. The ultimate annual payment would have been £1,240,673.

<small>Select Committee on Water Supply, 1880.</small> In June, 1880, a Select Committee was appointed to inquire into and to report upon the whole question of the London water supply, and upon the Agreements which had formed the basis of the Bill of 1880. The Committee reported that it was expedient that the supply of water to the metropolis should be placed under the control of some public body representing the interests and commanding the confidence of the water consumers. They recommended that "in the absence of any single municipal body" to which the control of the water supply could be committed, a new body should be constituted as a Water Authority for the Metropolis. The suggested composition of this body included representatives from the City Corporation, the Board of Works, and the districts of the Water Companies outside the metropolitan area. The Committee considered that the agreements of 1880 did not furnish "an admissible basis of purchase." The price agreed to be paid under these agreements was nine millions in excess of the market value of the property at a period shortly anterior, and several millions above their price at the time of the Committee's report. After

indicating the provisions for regulation, which had been made in the somewhat analogous case of the gas companies, they pointed out that the total cost of the existing water supply had not much exceeded £12,000,000, and that much of this was due to useless or re-duplicated works. They recommended that a future water authority should be entrusted with the fullest discretion as to the best method of dealing with the water supply of London, and they pointed out that such authority might proceed either by the regulation of the powers of existing companies, as in the case of the gas supply : or by the purchase of the existing undertakings : or by the initiation of an independent supply, there being no pretence for the contention that the companies had any sort of monopoly of supply.

The session of 1881 passed over without an opportunity being available to bring the London water supply question before the House of Commons. The crucial difficulty to be encountered in case of the introduction of such a Bill as was suggested by the Committee was the constitution of the Water Authority. It is doubtful whether it would be possible to constitute a Trust which would have the confidence of the consumers. With the very wide discretion suggested by the Committee, it would evidently be enormously to the interest of the Water Companies that the solution of the question should take the form of purchase and not the form either of regulation or of the institution of an independent supply. In a matter where many millions are at stake, the tendency to influence elections or nominations would be perhaps irresistible, and the people of London might thus be saddled with an enormous liability by some body of persons who could not be regarded as representing their interests. The risk of this is too great to be encountered. *Water Trust: Difficulty of Constitution.*

And yet the matter demands early solution. Some of the water companies have taken advantage of the delay to largely increase their rates on the consumer where only the same amount of water is supplied. This is technically within their *Water Supply under new Corporation.*

powers, owing to increased valuation and to such valuation being the accepted evidence of value upon which water rates are levied. The only security for a proper settlement of this vital question lies in referring it to a directly-elected body, representing the whole metropolis; and there would probably be no more difficulty in constituting such a body than there would be in constituting a Water Trust. All the methods of dealing with the question would then be fully considered, and a settlement arrived at, which, in the opinion of a truly representative body, would be to the advantage of their constituents.

Water Companies: Income and Expenditure.

The total capital of the eight water companies in August, 1881, was £12,536,988, the total money expended on works, £12,612,589, but many of these works have been unproductive, and in the time of the water wars some years ago, three competing sets of pipes were sometimes laid in the same street. The total receipts of the water companies in the previous year amounted to £1,534,939 of which the receipts from water rates were £1,515,194. The expenditure for the same period was £1,553,429. Of this there was paid in dividends on share capital, £771,575, and in dividends on loan and preference capital, £150,310. The maintenance and pumping charges were £248,747, salaries, £75,067, and allowance to directors, £22,794.

London Gas Supply.

The lighting of the streets of the town, whether by gas or electricity, is essentially a municipal function. It must be undertaken by the inhabitants acting in concert. Three hundred years ago, on the threat of a Spanish invasion, every London householder was bound to have a light before his door at night under penalty of death by the common hangman. One hundred and thirty years later the omission to supply such a light was punished by fine. From 1736 to the introduction of gas in 1810, the work in London was undertaken by the Corporation, who levied a special tax for the purpose. During the first half of the present century the competition between

London gas companies was very severe, and in some cases four companies had mains in the same street. But, as Viscount Ebrington pointed out in a letter to Lord Palmerston in 1854, " rival companies will always be found to coalesce for the plunder rather than compete for the cheap supply," and after exhausting themselves in conflict the companies agreed to divide the town amongst them. The raising of prices followed, until in 1857 the vestries met to take action against the common enemy, but found the companies too strong and too exacting or them, and the charges for public lamps (varying from £3 1s. 6d. to £6 16s.) still continued.

The first successful attempt at any sort of control was made after two committees had sat upon the question, by the passing of the Gas Act of 1860. This Act recognised a system of districting, and dealt with questions of dividend, quality, price, forms of yearly accounts, and other matters. With some advantages to the consumer, it enormously enhanced the value of the companies' property. If any Authority had existed able to speak in the consumers' name a better result must have been secured. In 1859 no company was able to declare a dividend of 10 per cent. In 1866, with a nominal capital of £5,863,130, the thirteen companies paid £530,357 in dividends. The companies paid up back dividends, and one of them divided 40 per cent. in a single year. The parishes were still charged varying prices for the same quality and amount of gas. In the ten years ending 1866 the companies expended £80,000 in the defence of their monopolies before Parliamentary committees. The London consumer, without any public body to represent him, was defeated at nearly every point, and an immense monopoly strengthened against his will. *Gas Act of 1860.*

The first effective attempt at a defence of the consumer was by the introduction of a Bill by the Corporation of London, in 1866, to enable the City to provide works for itself. The Bill was read a second time, and referred to a Select Committee, which reported strongly in favour of *Action of Corporation of London.*

alteration, in favour of the consumer, and in favour of facilities being afforded for the disposal of the companies' property to some body representing the consumer. The action of the City in introducing this measure was public-spirited and patriotic. The Metropolitan Board of Works actually petitioned against it, and they also petitioned against a Bill which had been introduced empowering them to purchase gas-works and plant. In other words, this so-called representative body used all its influence to prevent legislation in favour of the London gas consumer. In 1867 Sir Stafford Northcote introduced a Bill to carry out the recommendations of the committee of 1866. This was referred to a committee, of which Mr. Cardwell was chairman, and this committee reported, amongst other things, that the "legitimate weapon to be resorted to" for the reduction of price to the consumer "is the enactment of an independent supply."

Unjustifiable action of Metropolitan Board.

The committee "recommended" and invited the City Corporation and the Metropolitan Board to present competing schemes to Parliament in 1868. The City Corporation accepted the invitation with patriotic alacrity. The Metropolitan Board, although pressed by the Government and by many deputations from the London public, declined to introduce a Bill; declined to seize a proffered opportunity to settle in the interests of London this vexed question for ever. No reason can be given for this monstrous course of procedure, except that which has been given in other equally inexplicable cases, that the members of the Board have been influenced by considerations which have not been known to the public. In the face of such a betrayal of public interests, the contemporary language of a paper representing parish interests may be forgiven when it says: "A more wanton neglect of their interests was never charged or proved against any body presuming to protect them. The Board has deliberately, apparently by preconcerted design, helped the gas companies to maintain their monopoly against the express wish of

Parliament. It is time we stirred ourselves to overturn this dumb idol, and establish an effective real municipality in its place, elected direct from the ratepayers, instead of being filtered through the vestries, the prey or dupe apparently by turn of every class of jobbers who thrive on their ignorance, their neglect, or their ludicrous vanity."

In 1868 the City came forward with a Bill, and a Bill was also introduced under the direction of Mr. Beal, a gentleman who by untiring energy and zeal has on this and many other London questions rendered the most essential services to the cause of municipal reform. The Board of Works reported against it. The Bills were referred to a committee, and in the result the City of London Gas Act, 1868, was passed. Owing to the *lâches* and misconduct of the Board of Works, the great privileges it conferred were at first confined to the City area and to the area of one of the companies supplying it. Its advantages were manifest when we say that it saved in the first year to the City, £82,500. In 1870 the Government promised their support to the Metropolitan Board if they would introduce a measure for the rest of London, but they again declined to do so. City of London Gas Act.

In 1875 a Bill was introduced to regulate the price of London gas and the dividends of the Companies, and its provisions were afterwards sanctioned by a committee presided over by Mr. Forster. In the following year the Companies accepted its main provisions. The interests of the public and the rights of the Companies have now been adjusted by an arrangement under which the profits of the gas companies vary inversely with the price at which the gas is supplied. Various amalgamations have taken place, and three out of the four Companies, with nine-tenths of the supply, are now under this arrangement. The dividend being taken at 10 per cent., and the initial price at 3s. 6d. in one company and 3s. 9d. in the two others, it is arranged that every increase of a penny in price over the initial price must be accompanied by a reduction of ¼ per cent. Present Conditions of London Gas Supply.

G 2

in dividend, and every reduction of a penny in price by an increase of a ¼ per cent. in dividend. The result has been extremely advantageous to the consumer.

<small>Gas Supply under a new Corporation.</small>
But with the establishment of a municipal authority it will be needful to consider the position of the Companies. A provision for the purchase of the gas plant under London streets was contained in 50 Geo. III. c. 163, s. 32, the first London Gas Act, and the circumstances of the gas supply point strongly to the necessity of a central authority having absolute street control. An attempt was made in 1864 to enforce compulsory use of subways, but the London Gas Companies successfully opposed it, on the ground that the leakage from their pipes would be most dangerous. But this leakage admittedly only arose from their defective system of pipe-joining. Shortly afterwards Southwark Street was made by the Metropolitan Board. Its pavement was a work of Roman beauty, and a commodious subway ran down the centre. As soon as it was completed a gas company came, and, disregarding the subway, tore up the granite and concrete from end to end, to lay its own pipes. Londoners as ratepayers paid for the making of the street, and as gas consumers they paid for its destruction.

<small>Gas Companies' Income and Expenditure.</small>
If the new Corporation purchased the plant within the metropolitan area, the Companies might continue to manufacture the gas, the supply of which the Corporation might put up to tender. Or the Corporation might purchase the existing companies. Or it might initiate an independent supply. Committees of the House of Commons have reported that "no monopoly has been granted to the companies which the House of Commons is bound to respect," that a "legitimate weapon for the reduction is the enactment of an independent supply," and the right is now unquestionable. Therefore a central council would have a right, after giving full consideration to the question, to take what course it might think fit. The present system is, however, so pronounced an improvement upon all

that have gone before it, and affords so comparatively strong a guarantee for the preservation of the public advantage, that the subject is less absolutely imminent than at previous times. If gas is an article of necessity to the people of London, then beyond doubt the true principle is that its supply should be in public hands. But scientific research is fast challenging the proposition that it is an article of necessity. If the progress of electric invention should proceed as rapidly in the next three years as in the last, the conditions of public and private lighting will be completely changed, and any central council would do well to wait until such time as such new conditions were fully developed.

During the year 1880 the London Gas Companies paid for coal £1,389,461. They carbonised 1,898,474 tons of coal, and produced 17,732 million feet of gas. Of this there was supplied for public lighting and under contracts about 1,100 million cubic feet, and more than 1,000 million feet were unaccounted for. The cost of distribution was £223,875, and the cost of management £118,280. The receipts were, from sales of gas £3,010,936, from meter-rents £57,991, and from the sale of residual products (coke, breeze, tar, and ammoniacal liquor) £908,526. The total receipts were £3,988,541.

Amalgamation has now reduced the number of London gas companies to four—the Gas Light and Coke Company, the South Metropolitan, the Commercial, and the London Gas Light Company. The total paid-up capital of these four companies was, on Dec. 31, 1880, £10,784,961. Of this the Gas Light and Coke Company had £7,515,000, the South Metropolitan £1,831,990, the Commercial £675,845, the London £762,126. There was a further authorised but unissued capital of £1,269,757, making a total authorised capital of £12,054,718. The loan account of the Companies shows £2,047,549 borrowed, and £1,302,805 authorised but not borrowed. The whole amount, therefore,

Gas Companies' Capital Account.

stands: capital paid up and loans issued, £12,832,510; further authorised capital and loans, £2,572,462.

CONSIDERATION OF REFORM. In the preceding pages we have set out the nature and extent of existing municipal and quasi-municipal jurisdictions in London. Their imperfect and non-representative character has been made manifest, and an endeavour has been made to show the urgent need of alteration, and the direction in each case which reform may most usefully take. It remains to consider how the grant of representative municipal institutions to London may be best carried into actual practice.

Grouping of Jurisdictions. The existing conditions of London government naturally group themselves under several heads. First, there are the municipal functions now discharged by private bodies, but which all people admit should be under a single metropolitan control. To this class belong the water and gas supply. Next come the municipal functions, which are now undertaken by some public authority, working from a single administrative centre. To this class belong the control of education by the London School Board; of the poor law by the Local Government Board; of sick poor by the Metropolitan Asylums Board; of the police force by the Home Office; of the Metropolitan rivers by the Conservancy Boards; the market jurisdiction of the City; and the special jurisdictions of the Metropolitan Board of Works, including, main drainage; Thames Embankment; Thames floods; bridges; Metropolitan improvements; parks, commons, and open spaces; fire brigade; supervision of streets and buildings; artizans' dwellings; inspection of dairies, cowsheds, and milk stores; inspection under the Explosives, Petroleum, Infant Life Protection, and Cattle Diseases Acts; certain powers under the Gas and Water Acts, and the control of slaughter-houses and offensive businesses.

Effect of Recent Legislation. It is to be noted that by far the larger number of the jurisdictions of the Metropolitan Board were confided to it by acts of the Legislature at a time when the vestries and district boards might have undertaken them if Parliament had considered these jurisdictions more adapted for local than central administration in London: and, having regard both to this original legislative selection, and to the fairly satisfactory manner in which central authorities have discharged the various duties now imposed upon them, it is not likely that any successful proposition could be made to again divide the control of these matters amongst central municipalities or independent local councils. It will moreover be noted that the two groups of jurisdictions above mentioned comprise by far the larger share of the municipal work of London.

The third group of existing municipal jurisdictions comprise those which are in the hands of local bodies as final authorities. The economical and practical advantages of having the ultimate control of these in the hands of a central authority have been pointed out when the jurisdictions themselves were under examination, but it is perhaps true that the efficient management of most of them would be advanced by having in some form the assistance and advice of the inhabitants of different localities. These jurisdictions include the control of streets (including paving, lighting, watering, cleansing, street cellars, footpaths, and crossings); the appointment of sanitary, nuisance, and food inspectors and medical officers; and the provision of baths and wash-houses, drinking fountains, public pumps, disinfecting chambers, mortuaries, cemeteries, and other matters. Nearly all these functions could be discharged equally well, as we have already shown, by a central authority, and most of them much better. *Vestry Jurisdictions under new Corporation.*

There remains another class of London jurisdiction which requires modification or abolition. This includes the jurisdiction of the Corporation of Westminster; of the Tower of London; of the county authorities; the judicial functions of aldermen; the legislative functions of the Court of Aldermen; the control of brokers' rents; the municipal functions of the Livery Companies; the coal and wine dues; and the grain duty. *Jurisdictions requiring change.*

We have already discussed the manner in which these may be most satisfactorily dealt with.

<small>Argument for a Single Central Authority.</small>
As to all municipal functions which might be best discharged in London by a central authority, it is scarcely necessary to point out that, for every purpose, it would be better that they should be under one central authority than as at present under many separate central authorities; and the whole scope of the argument, therefore, points to the necessity of establishing a central representative municipal authority, controlling all administration and all expenditure. Long before the practicability of such a solution had been illustrated by the action of the central bodies we have named, the Municipal Commissioners of 1837 had stated in their report that they failed "to find any argument on which the course pursued with regard to other towns could be justified, which would not apply with the same force to London, unless the magnitude of the change in this case should be considered as converting that which would otherwise be only a practical difficulty into an objection of principle." The logic of events has solved the "practical difficulty," so far as some of the most intricate matters of municipal control are concerned. As to the alternative suggestion which has sometimes been made, for the establishment of separate municipalities, they say, "We hardly anticipate that it will be suggested, for the purpose of removing the appearance of singularity, that the other quarters of the town should be formed into independent and isolated communities, if, indeed, the multifarious relations to which their proximity compels them would permit them to be isolated and independent. This plan would, as it seems to us, in getting rid of an anomaly tend to multiply and perpetuate an evil."

<small>Opinion of Commissioners of 1837 and 1854.</small>
Their exhaustive examination into the conditions of London Government and the singular success which has attended the Municipal Corporations Act, give to the opinions of the Commissioners peculiar value. The opinion was nevertheless subsequently contested. The three Commissioners

appointed to collect information with respect to, and make recommendations as to, the Government of the City of London, who reported in 1854, went outside the scope of their commission, and, adopting the opinions of some of the City witnesses called before them, suggested the constitution for London of a series of municipalities, with a central authority, to be composed of deputies from each. The suggested functions of this central authority were confined to the management of public works of metropolitan importance, the plans for which should be previously submitted for the sanction of the Privy Council.

The Metropolitan Board of Works was constituted in the following year, with functions somewhat wider than those which the Commissioners had suggested, and since that time this body has undertaken departments of municipal work which the Commissioners considered could not be safely confided to a central authority. Events have, therefore, removed much of the value which the opinions of the Commissioners might have at one time possessed, and indeed, as the matter was outside their reference, these opinions were never more than *obiter dicta*, and as the Commissioners candidly enough say, the form of such outside municipalities was not one upon which they were " competent to express any opinion "! Moreover, the suggested municipalities were never constituted.

As the present City authorities and representatives are endeavouring to represent this Commission as reporting favourably to the continuance of the City as at present, it may be useful to quote the language used by the City in a manifesto put forth under its authority, when Sir Geo. Grey introduced his Bill in 1856, founded on this report. They say, " The Government Bill, a Bill of pains and penalties, is doubly unconstitutional. In principle it is at variance with the fundamental law of the realm, as defined by Lord Coke, and it has for its basis the *Report of a body who not only came to the enquiry with prejudice, and reported against evidence, but who were themselves unconstitutionally appointed for purposes of aggression and legislation, and who conducted their proceedings in illegal form !"*

Mr. Ayrton's Committee.

The Local Government and Taxation Committee of 1867 recommended that the Metropolitan Board be erected into a Municipal Council, to be composed of members elected, partly by Local Councils in various districts of the metropolis, partly by direct election from the ratepayers, with a third portion to be selected from the justices of the metropolis, as representing property owners—and with two members nominated by the Crown on account of the rating of Crown property. The Local Councils suggested by this committee were to be directly elected governors of newly adjusted areas, and to take over the functions of the vestries and District Boards. The powers of the Municipal Council were to be more extensive than those of the Metropolitan Board, and included the control of the gas and water supply, and the custody of public interests affecting railways and other undertakings within the metropolis.

Argument from Recent Legislation.

The recommendations of this committee were never effectuated by legislation, but the establishment of the London School Board in 1870, and the constant grant of fresh powers to the Metropolitan Board, have strongly advanced the principle of undivided municipal control, until, in recent years, municipal reformers have completely endorsed the opinion expressed by the *Times* in October, 1874, that "whatever may be the plan adopted it is certain that by some means or other the whole of London must be brought under the same government. We have already too long suffered from the necessary want of unity and co-operation between the two bodies which administer our affairs. It is time now that this was at an end, and it can be ended only by the creation of one Municipal Government for all London, under which London may take worthily the rank to which she is entitled."

Separate Municipalities.

The separate municipality idea, with its ten mayors and hundreds of aldermen and thousands of councillors, may therefore be dismissed. Whenever it has been advanced in the form of a Bill in Parliament it has met with City opposition, although in later years the authorities of the Corporation have viewed it with a more friendly eye, as furnishing the only means of preserving intact their estates and privileges in the presence of any irresistible demand for reform. If such a scheme were ever carried out, the conflict of jurisdictions, of interests, and of authority would produce a metropolitan chaos even beyond that which we have delineated. Eleven different rating authorities would divide London amongst them, and the most expert statesman would be puzzled to say what jurisdiction should be given to the central body and what to the local bodies. These latter, moreover, would require even more constituting than a central authority, and would interfere more with existing authorities at the time of transition. The number of men to whom the Mayoralty of Islington or the Aldermanry of Bethnal Green would be an object of ambition, would be small. Neither would such a system result in the preservation to the City area of their cherished privileges and property.

The two arguments most persistently advanced against the establishment of a unified system of municipal government in London are, first: that it is impossible for a central municipality to properly supervise an infinity of detail over so vast an area; and, second, that the legislature would not consent to the establishment of so powerful a body—an *imperium in imperio*—at its own doors. As to the first of these objections, it has been answered, as we have shown, by the logic of events. The Metropolitan Board in the execution of the Building Acts, and the School Board, in the execution of the Education Act, do, from single centres, control matters of the closest detail affecting the habitations and the lives of the people. No other branches of municipal work, except the administration of the Poor Law, approach these in the personal and local detail involved. Nor would the detail work of such a municipality be so extensive as that of a great railway company, like the London and North-Western; or a private association, like the

Objections to Single Municipality.

Western Union Telegraph Company of America; or of various departments of the State, as, for example, the Post Office, under the control of much smaller bodies of men.

Objection to Magnitude.
As to the second objection, it is one rather of prejudice than of practice. When Sir Benjamin Hall's Bill was under discussion in 1855, it was suggested that the Board of Works might discuss politics rather than sewage, and, perhaps, overshadow the authority of the Imperial Parliament. No such result has ensued. With a series of municipalities it is quite likely that the borough political organisations might control elections within their own area, but that is not so feasible or likely with smaller electoral and administrative areas, and a central municipality. With co-terminous areas, provincial Corporations are often swayed by the politics of the borough over which they rule, but the circumstances of London under a single municipality would be widely different. If, however, these arguments are found to be of common acceptance, and if the Legislature hesitate to endow a London municipality with the vast control to which it is entitled, a *via media* might be found in the creation of a responsible Minister for London, who should have the conduct of the Municipality Bills in Parliament, and through whom the Legislature might continue to exercise such control as was deemed necessary. The concession of the powers sought is imperative, and, in our judgment, they might be safely and wisely given without such reciprocal parliamentary control; but it is better to have the latter than to be denied the former.

Methods of Creation: Municipality Bill 1880.
In the creation of a municipality for London, there are two courses open for adoption. The first is that which was illustrated by the Municipality of London Bill, 1880. The object of that measure was the creation of a new municipality, to consist of a lord mayor, forty aldermen, and two hundred municipal councillors. The metropolis was divided into forty districts, each of which sent five councillors and one alderman to the council. The elections were triennial, and there were provisions whereby some of the City aldermen and the members of

the Metropolitan Board and of the vestries should be upon the first council. There was also a power in the council of nominating local assistants, if necessary.

To the council so constituted was transferred the functions, powers, authorities, and property of the corporation of the City, the Metropolitan Board, the vestries, district boards, and other bodies. The Bill contained many elaborate provisions for the retention of old servants, the apportionment of county property, and other necessary matters. The mode of procedure adopted was both logical and practical, and the Bill might be regarded as a scheme to establish a perfect municipal ideal at a single effort. *Details of Bill of 1880.*

The central council would, as in other corporations, have exercised its control through committees, and probably one representative of each district would have been found on the most important of such committees where local matters had to be dealt with. There would be such a division of work as would enable business men to attend. The system of direct personal responsibility would be applied to the mechanical part of municipal works, so that, under the best available men, each department of work would be performed in the most efficient manner. Separate committees for drainage, water supply, gas supply, police, education, poor relief, public works, public property, public health, extinction of fire, taxation assessment and finance, law and parliamentary work, audit, and special purposes, would have had entrusted to them the whole municipal work of the town, and there is no room for doubt but that, under such an arrangement, it might be most effectively done. *Procedure of Municipality under Bill of 1880.*

But the establishment of so much that was new would necessarily involve the extinction or merger of much that was old; and if a responsible Administration should undertake the work of London reform, it would probably prefer a less rapid rate of progress. If, therefore, some means could be devised for bridging over the great change, and some scheme *Methods of Creation: Procedure by Adaptation of existing Systems.*

settled which, whilst utilising to the utmost, existing forces, should yet leave the new organisation full scope to perfect itself, it would no doubt be more acceptable to what is known as practical statesmanship.

<small>Extension of Corporation of City of London.</small> Adopting this position, and building the new edifice on the old foundations, it may be at once admitted that, if it were possible to use and extend the framework of the existing Corporation of London over the whole metropolis, much would be done towards facilitating the settlement of the question, and also towards lessening the opposition of persons who would regret anything which amounted to a destruction of the historic continuity of London corporate life. If the extension of the existing Corporation involved an adoption or a probable reproduction of its procedure or its internal character, it would be better to wait fifty years for reform than carry out such a proposition.

<small>Character of City Institutions.</small> But, putting out of sight its present working, the machine itself is a noble one. Linked through long centuries in the past with every cause of public freedom and of public liberty, the City has been careful to preserve for itself the benefits of free corporate institutions; and, if it were possible to infuse a new and vigorous municipal life into those institutions, by extending them over the whole metropolitan area, it is probable that statesmen would prefer such a course of procedure to a proposition which, however excellent and practical in itself, constructs everything anew. As it is a Corporation that is to be established, it is manifestly better, if we are to utilise one or other of existing institutions, that we should utilise the Corporation of London rather than the Metropolitan Board of Works. In the latter case, we should have to constitute anew the various forms of corporate government; whilst in the former we have the machinery ready to our hand.

<small>Amalgamation of Board of Works and City.</small> Nor would there be very serious difficulties to encounter in carrying such a proposition out. It would be necessary to effect a union, under controlling authority, of the various duties which

the Metropolitan Board and the City now discharge concurrently. The practice pursued by the City of requiring the exclusion of the City area whenever authorities were given to the Metropolitan Board, has had the result of necessitating the constitution of separate committees in the City, for the purpose of controlling such subjects. Thus the staff working under the present Commissioners of Sewers and under the Works and General Purposes Committee of the Board of Works, might each be put under the control of the Commissioners of Sewers until such time as the new council might examine into the position of that Commission, and decide upon what ought to be its future relation to the Corporation.

The same observation applies to the amalgamation of the Bridge House Estates' Committee of the City, and the Bridges' Committee of the Metropolitan Board. The well-known Coal, Corn, and Finance Committee of the City Corporation would also undertake in the new council the work hitherto done by the Finance Committee of the Board of Works. The Epping Forest Committee of the City would be reconstituted, and take the work of the Parks, Commons, and Open Spaces Committee of the Metropolitan Board. As to the work now done by the Fire Brigade Committee and the Building Acts Committee of the Metropolitan Board, these committees would have to be reconstituted as committees of the Central Council. *Committee Amalgamation.*

These illustrations sufficiently indicate the comparative ease with which the staff and functions of the one body might be united to the other. At first, all the city committees would probably be retained. The City Lands; Markets; Police; City of London School; Officers and Clerks; Improvement; Orphan School; Law and City Courts; Local Government and Taxation; and Grain Committee, might all continue the matters now controlled by the committees of the existing Corporation, and such other matters of the same kind throughout the metropolitan area as should be entrusted to the new Corporation. The Library Committee might continue the control over *Retention of City Committees.*

the City Library, and also consider the whole question of Free Libraries and Museums throughout the metropolis. Under the Public Libraries Acts the consent of the majority of ratepayers in a district is now requisite. This consent is rarely given by reason of the cost, but probably there would, under a new Corporation, be endowments available for the purpose. As the City now undertakes within its own borders all the work which is done in outer London by the vestries, the committees under whose direction such work is now performed would supply the initial organisation for carrying it out throughout London. It was proposed in Mr. Buxton's Bills to have a permanent Chairman of Committees. The existing staff of officers attached to vestries and district boards would probably be retained in the first instance with their present duties, but acting subject to the central committee and probably under skilled control.

Facility of Transition. A system so established would disturb to the least possible extent existing institutions. The framework of the City Corporation providing for the control of nearly every class of municipal work would leave very little requiring absolutely new creation. The only material change would be in the nature of the controlling authorities. It might even be confidently expected that, from all parts of London, would come up, elected by the people, the best representative men now working in the vestries and in other organisations—men who are familiar with the work done by those bodies in the past and who would thus preserve to the greatest possible extent the continuity of public work.

Power of complete Internal Reform. Constituted thus in the first instance on city lines, the new Corporation would no doubt apply itself, at an early period, to the question of internal reform; and its work in this direction would be facilitated by the possession of a power now in the hands of the Common Council, and which would of course survive to the new body. By a charter of 15 King Edward the Third (included for Parliamentary confirmation in the 2 William and

Mary, sess. 1, c. 3,) it is provided "that if any customs hitherto used and obtained in the city shall be bad or defective, or if any matters newly arising within the city shall need amendment, where no remedy shall have been previously provided," such remedy may be applied by the government of the City, provided it be agreeable to good faith and reason (*congruum bonæ fidei et rationi consonum*) and useful to king and people. The Municipal Corporations Act, 1835, only empowers the enactment of bye-laws, and no such power of internal legislation is possessed by any other corporation. Whilst its existence emphasises the reproach which attaches to existing City abuses, it at the same time will furnish to a new Corporation immense and necessary advantages in placing its constitution upon satisfactory lines.

The area over which the jurisdiction of the Corporation would at first be extended would be that included in the Metropolis Management Act, 1855. This area covers 75,490 acres, with 488,995 houses; a population of 3,832,441, and a net rateable value in April, 1881, of £27,847,875. This area is somewhat larger than that of the united Parliamentary Boroughs, and considerably less than that of the London police district. The settlement of the best metropolitan boundary would be a matter which would receive the early attention of a new Corporation. The present boundary includes large areas of country districts in the neighbourhood of Woolwich and Lewisham, and excludes densely populated contiguous districts like West Ham. *Area of new Corporation.*

Coming next to internal division, it may be admitted that electoral and administrative areas ought to be coterminous. It is not difficult to construct an ideal division of London into forty wards, with an approximate population of 100,000 each. A map showing such divisions was annexed to the Municipality of London Bill, 1880. *Division of Area in Bill of 1880.*

If, however, the settlement of areas should be left to the subsequent action of the Corporation, there would be no great difficulty in proceeding in the first instance on existing lines. *Temporary acceptance of existing Areas.*

H

The feasibility of doing this was illustrated by a bill introduced by Earl Camperdown into the House of Lords in 1877. The object of the bill was to increase the number of members of the Metropolitan Board of Works to 100, and to alter the mode of their election. These 100 members were divided amongst the present local areas in proportion to their population. The larger parishes had six, five, or four members respectively, and the smaller vestries and district boards three, two, or one, as the case might be. The retention of the present vestry divisions in a new system would in any case be only a tentative arrangement. They differ infinitely in every respect; they cross and interlace each other in bewildering confusion. Some times one vestry bisects another, as St. George's, Hanover Square, bisects Westminster Board of Works. At other times the parts of a parish are widely separated, as Kensal town is two miles distant from the rest of the parish of Chelsea. In some places the roadway belongs to one vestry, and the footpath to another. In other cases the dividing line passes down the centre of a street, and each vestry paves to the middle.

Division of Representation in existing Areas.

The settlement of boundaries and areas for all purposes would probably be the subject of an enquiry at an early period after the constitution of the council. If, however, in the first instance the existing boundaries were preserved, it would not be difficult to divide the members of the new Corporation amongst existing areas according to the population, or, as was suggested by the Taxation Committee of 1867, according to population and rateable value. Whether the latter should be ultimately retained as an element of representation, the Corporation itself might decide. Under the Metropolis Local Management Act, 1855, the number of vestrymen is apportioned according to the number of rated householders, and in settling the number of vestrymen for wards both population and rateable value are to be considered. (18 & 19 Vict. c. 120, ss. 2, 3.) Under such a temporary arrangement, there would be no injustice in giving the

City area in the first instance twenty-five members—that is to say, one for each ward now electing Common Councillors. Judging from a recent enquiry, it is extremely doubtful whether, of the whole 232 members of the present Common Council there are as many as twenty-five having a residential address within the City. The rest might very fairly, therefore, present themselves as candidates in the parts of London where they live, if their municipal ambition survived the extension of the present Corporation. With respect to the Metropolitan Board of Works, it would, beyond doubt, be useful to have men experienced in the municipal work of Spring Gardens on the new Council; and if (excluding the City) the thirty-six areas now electing the Board were taken as the basis of the first election, there would be no insuperable objection to admitting thirty-six of the present members of the Board as *ex officio* councillors from these districts, and lessening the proportion to be elected by this number. It might also be practicable, if desired, to have thirty-eight vestrymen nominated by the thirty-eight existing jurisdictions as *ex officio* members of the first Council. The second municipal election would be on the new lines, settled after a public enquiry, but under some such system as this the first Council would have, for three years, the benefit of municipal experience of much value, and probably such a scheme would be better than one which proposed simply to increase the numbers of the first Council by the members of the Metropolitan Board or other bodies as *ex officio* councillors.

The population and rateable value of the various divisions of London are set out in the table at the end of this paper. In the final apportionment of representation the City will be made the subject of special treatment. If 240 members were divided through London according to population, the unit would be 16,000 to each, and the City would have three members; if according to rateable value, the unit would be £116,000, and the City would have 30 members; if both were considered, it

Special treatment of City.

might have 15. It is almost devoid of the ordinary municipal population. Of 50,276 persons who may be found at night in 6,418 houses, the great majority are caretakers, and four-fifths are women and children. It is, therefore, a huge aggregation of offices and warehouses to which people come in the morning, and which they leave at night. Only a very small proportion of these persons ever interfere with municipal matters in the City. These are controlled by a small body of men, most of whom come from outer London, and some of whom have only a "brass-plate qualification" in the City. The Corporation is, therefore, a non-resident body, but in order to "retain its individual existence as a separate municipality" it has recently expended over £1,000 in taking what is termed a "Day Census." On April 25, 1881, in 24 hours, nearly 800,000 persons entered the City, or crossed some portion of it. Many thousands of these were counted several times over, and if the Strand district or Southwark were so counted, their population would be increased many times; and to the population of Hitchin would have to be added all the passengers by Great Northern trains passing through it. Perhaps one-sixth of the cabs and omnibuses in London enter the City in a day, but according to this census the number was considerably larger than the whole number existing. As it is the custom of Londoners to make their income-tax returns in the City, these are carefully added up and found to be nearly equal to the rest of London, and apparently serious arguments advanced thereon.

Day Census of City.

But the most elaborate arguments and comparative tables are based upon what is stated to be the true population of the City—261,061. This is composed of 57,503, "all of whom are employers of labour," 162,253 "residing daily within its walls and paying their share of its taxes," 20,000 women caretakers and domestic servants, and 21,305 children. The last two classes belong mainly to the night population. The 162,253 are "clerks," "warehousemen," "assistants," "porters," "shoeblacks," &c. These persons have neither vote nor interest in the City. They are less concerned in it than the millhands who fill the Lancashire mills by day and go elsewhere at night are concerned with the districts where the mills are. In the years 1871-81 Manchester has decreased in population 2·8, whilst Salford has increased 41·2, but on the City basis of calculation much of the Salford population ought also to be counted in Manchester! In the City census tables these 162,253 are counted twice over, once in the City and a second time in the London boroughs, with which the City is compared!

Nor is the estimate of 57,503 "employers of labour" more reliable. For example, there are entered 2,616 barristers in the Temple. It is safe to say that not one-third of the number ever were in the Temple on any given day, and many hundreds of them live in the provinces and elsewhere. Testing the matter from a municipal point of view, it is probably true that not one-tenth of the whole 2,616 know in what City ward they live, or who "represents" them on the Common Council, and not one-twentieth ever voted in a City municipal election. The City census is, therefore, peculiarly unreliable and misleading, but it is useful as showing the absence of the ordinary conditions of municipal life in the City area. As the population claimed for the City mainly both live and vote outside, it is quite open to argument whether this area ought not to be administered by the new Corporation as the heritage of the whole municipality.

<small>Misleading Character of Day Census</small>

The total number of the new Council might be usefully settled at 240, including Aldermen, but exclusive of the Lord Mayor. The Common Council of the City at present numbers 232. Its number was condemned as far too large both by the Commissioners of 1837 and 1854. It is now still more disproportionate. The Board of Works does half the municipal work of London with forty-five members, but they are very much overworked. The London School Board has fifty members, and the Metro-

<small>Numbers of new Corporation.</small>

politan Asylums Board sixty members. If Lord Camperdown's suggested increase of the Metropolitan Board of Works to 100 had been carried out, there would have been an approximately true relation between the work to be done and the men to do it. If the number of the present Common Council were extended from 232 to 240, there is no reason to suppose that the work imposed upon them would prove unduly burdensome, or would prevent the municipality from securing the services of the best class of men. This number might ultimately be divided amongst forty areas, or in such other manner as the Council should think fit.

Aldermen of New Corporation.

In whatever form the two hundred councillors were afterwards distributed, it is probable that the forty aldermen would be the recognised municipal heads of as many districts in London. But, for the purpose of an initial and tentative measure, it might not be unjust to make the eight City aldermen who have not passed the chair *ex officio* aldermen of the new Corporation. This might either be done by having forty-four aldermen in the first instance (one for each of the thirty-six Board electoral areas, and eight for the City), or by having only forty, but dividing the thirty-two then remaining amongst the thirty-six existing electoral areas, by combining eight of the smaller areas into four, for the purpose of electing aldermen, as Lewisham is now joined with Plumstead, and Rotherhithe with St. Olave for the purpose of electing two members of the Metropolitan Board of Works.

How to deal with existing Vestries.

A much more difficult problem to solve, is how to deal with the vestries and district boards now existing. With all their evils and disadvantages, and the waste consequent upon their want of concerted action, the London vestries have done and are doing a vast amount of municipal work, and much of it they are doing well. If a central council of 240 members were constituted, and the municipal work of the town confided to them without local assistance, they could probably manage it just as well as a board of directors of a great railway company can control effectually thousands of men and millions of money.

But it may be forcibly urged, that in such an event the help of many hundreds of men now devoting their services usefully to the public would be lost, and ultimately the central Council itself might suffer from the want of any previous municipal experience in the men elected to it. In addition to this, there would be a great advantage to the community in enlisting the interest and assistance of a considerable number of citizens in the government of the town, if such assistance could be available without detriment to the working of a new municipal system. As Mr. Mill has said, "Whatever might be the case in some other constitutions of society, the spirit of a commercial people will be, we are persuaded, essentially mean and slavish whenever public spirit is not cultivated by an extensive participation of the people in the business of government in detail; nor will the desideratum of a general diffusion of intelligence among either the middle or lower classes be realised but by a corresponding dissemination of public functions and a voice in public affairs." *[margin: Disadvantage of complete Extinction of Vestries]*

If it were practicable to constitute a number of local bodies analogous to the present vestries, with independent functions, or even to establish ten London municipalities, they would infallibly suffer from all the disadvantages attaching to some of the vestries, and they would not offer a legitimate ambition to men anxious to assist in public work. As Mr. Mill has well said, "It is quite hopeless to induce persons of a high class, either socially or intellectually, to take a share of local administration in a corner by piecemeal as members of a paving board or a drainage commission. The entire local business of their town is not more than a sufficient object to induce men whose tastes incline them and whose knowledge qualifies them for national affairs, to become members of a mere local body, and devote to it the time and study which are necessary to render their presence more than a *[margin: Disadvantages of independent Local Councils.]*

screen for the jobbing of inferior persons under the shelter of their responsibility."

Local Councils as part of new Corporation.
But if such bodies were part of a great municipal system, and were endowed with functions for active work to be discharged in common with the aldermen and councillors of the districts, the result would be different, and the membership of such bodies would be regarded as a valuable training for, and stepping-stone to, a higher municipal position in the council itself. In this view of the case it might be advisable, if possible, to constitute in each metropolitan area a local body to advise and assist the Council in its general municipal work, and to discharge such duties as may be delegated to it by the Central Council; and Mr. M. H. Levirton, who has given much study to this subject, has suggested that such a body might be able to render much local assistance, and meeting monthly with the central councillors of the district, and under the presidency of the alderman of the ward, might deliberate on the affairs and requirements of the district, and thus ensure their full recognition by the central authority.

Numbers and Functions of Local Councils.
The number of such a body might depend in the first instance upon the size of the local area, and might afterwards be settled by the council. It might render service in receiving, considering, and making reports affecting the water and gas supply of the district, and might make, through the councillors, representations either as to the further requirements of the locality or as to the whole system. Where its jurisdiction abutted on the river, it might consider matters affecting floods, embankment, and bridges, so that the central council would know through the councillors for the district what the views of the locality were. The whole system of inspection—medical, sanitary, food, nuisance, and other, might be usefully checked and controlled. As to street control, such bodies might recommend alterations in paving or lighting, and probably, subject to engineering and other practical considerations, the opinion of the local body would carry much weight. The desirability of establishing libraries, mortuaries, disinfecting chambers, and

baths and washhouses, would carefully be first considered in such a council, and its opinion would also be of value on the greater questions of street improvements, public parks, artizans' dwellings, fire brigade stations, and so forth. They might also supply the members of assessment committees, if the council should so decide. In the first instance the present vestry halls might be utilised for the meetings of the local body.

The highest type of Municipal Government in London will be that which unites effective general and extended local control. It is, perhaps, hardly to be expected that a Government measure would, in the first instance, give either the educational or poor law administration of the town to a new municipality. But both would probably come as soon as the Legislature found that a reliable and responsible body of citizens had undertaken the control of municipal affairs. The control of educational expenditure ought to be given at once to the new Corporation, and when the municipality had also the control of educational work, the importance and usefulness of these local bodies would be largely increased, and they would supply the School Managers and Divisional Committees. As to the administration of the poor law, the Local Government and Taxation Committee of 1867 expressed the opinion that in order to avoid multiplicity of authorities, and in order to promote efficiency of administration combined with economy, the Board of Guardians should be merged in the municipal authority. The conclusion was both just and practical, and by simply increasing their number the Local Councils could well undertake the duties now discharged by Boards of Guardians, whilst the Central Council would frame the regulations and undertake the general control to which we have alluded in our observations on the poor law. With these added jurisdictions, the Local Councils might become a most important element in the Municipal Government of London. *Ultimate Functions of Local Councils.*

The Municipality of London Bill, 1880, recognised the position to the extent of providing for the nomination of local assistants in the same way that School Board managers are *Election of Municipal Councillors, &c.*

nominated, but it left such nomination optional with the council, and also relegated to the council the definition of the functions of such local assistants. It has, however, been considered that the usefulness of school managers would have been enhanced if they had been the subject of popular election, and undoubtedly the tendency of modern opinion is in the direction of elected rather than nominated bodies for the administration of all departments of municipal work.

<small>Tenure of Office.</small>

The tenure of office of all the members of the Corporation might be three years. No useful object would be served by disturbing the metrópolis by such a yearly election of councillors as now takes place in the City, or by the system under which one-third go out each year. The experience of the School Board has shown that a triennial election of all the members of a public body always results in the return of a sufficiently large number of old members to leave the continuity of public work undisturbed, whilst the example of the Imperial Government goes still further in the same direction. There is no good reason why this rule should not be applied to all classes of municipal rulers in London, except, of course, the Lord Mayor. He would be elected yearly by the council, but be eligible for re-election, and the field of choice would be extended so as to include every citizen of the metropolis.

<small>Suggested Method of Election of Aldermen, Councillors, and Local Councillors.</small>

If such a system were adopted, the triennial election would not be difficult to arrange, and, as suggested by the Taxation Committee of 1867, the election to all municipal offices should take place on the same day. If, for example, we had a district where there were to be elected one alderman, five councillors, and a fixed number of local councillors, the voting paper might contain three divisions. In the first would be the candidates nominated for the post of alderman; in the second the candidates nominated as councillors; and in the third the candidates nominated as local councillors; and any candidate might be nominated in two or all of the three divisions. Every elector would be entitled to vote for one person in the first division, for five in the second, and for the number to be elected in the third. The alderman votes would first be counted. The candidate receiving the highest number would be alderman of the district for the next three years. Next the councillor votes would be counted, after striking out all the votes given to the elected alderman—if he should have also been nominated a councillor—and the five highest be elected, and so on with the third division. It would probably not be needful in these elections to give minorities the cumulative vote, but in suffrage, method, and charge of election, the present School Board system might be adopted.

The course of action just considered is rather the development of institutions which exist than the creation of an edifice new from foundation to coping. It will probably commend itself much more readily to those who deprecate revolutionary change. But the necessity for some change, and the direction which it ought to take, have now been fully considered. Whilst the defects and imperfections of London government may be found in every department of it, they are most manifest in the districts of the town where good sanitary and municipal administration is most required. We have preferred, however, to rest the case for reform less upon deficiencies arising out of existing systems than on the deficiencies of the systems themselves. With the material available for the purpose, it would have been an easy but withal an invidious task to enforce a demand for reform by illustrations of the manner in which, under existing systems, personal considerations often take precedence of the public good. But we have preferred to rest our case upon the defects of the system itself, and upon the inherent rights of the London people. The capital has been held back in the grip of vested interests, and although, in the conduct of her rulers, she has never approached the hideous experience of New York twenty years ago, she has, on the other hand, never given any illustration of that genius for local self-government which the Municipal Corporations Act of 1835 has done so much to evoke.

Case for Reform.

Future of London under United Municipal System.

But under a unified municipal system like that here indicated, we might hope that the capital would rapidly advance to take its true position amongst English municipalities. It was the complaint of the Commissioners of 1837 that "the highest classes of commercial men do not ordinarily take a share in the management of the Corporation, and a large proportion who might, if they pleased, take an important part in the Corporation felt a repugnance to doing so." This complaint was echoed by the Commissioners of 1854, and it would not be too much to say that the *probi homines* sent up by the wards to advise the City aldermen in the time of King Edward the First occupied a more representative position in the City than the aldermen themselves do to-day. Under a new Corporation we might expect to see this state of things changed. There are in London many thousands of men with leisure, ability, and wide experience who would readily place themselves at the service of the community, and who would bring to it a judgment, a distinction, and a knowledge of affairs which would be of great value. The commercial and trading classes would send representatives of the kind whose absence the Commissioners deplored; the best of our present rulers would be found taking their seats in the council; and, lastly, we might hope for the presence of men understanding the interests and possessing the confidence of London artisans.

Conclusion. A Corporation so constituted would rapidly enlist the confidence both of Londoners and of Parliament. The former would find their interests safe-guarded, and their city intelligently ruled, whilst the latter would be relieved from an enormous incubus of London work which now occupies its time, and which it is but imperfectly qualified to discharge. With unified, systematic, and representative municipal government the citizens of London would soon learn to take a pride in their city, and, acting together on common lines for the "common profit of the people"—as the old charters run—would soon elevate her to the position which she is justly fitted to occupy, as the Head of the Municipalities of the World.

AND HOW TO REFORM IT. 125

THE POPULATION, INHABITED HOUSES, AND RATEABLE VALUE OF LONDON WITHIN THE METROPOLIS LOCAL MANAGEMENT ACT, 1855.

	Population.	Inhabited Houses.	Rateable Annual Value.
City of London...	50,276	6,418	£3,500,968
Vestries, under the Metropolis Local Management Act, 1855:—			
Marylebone	155,004	16,021	1,383.987
Pancras	236,209	24,655	1,491,461
Lambeth	253,569	35,082	1,284,862
St. George's, Hanover Square	89,517	11,593	1,679,299
Islington	282,628	34,048	1,445.226
Shoreditch	126,565	15,243	576,782
Paddington	107,098	13,187	1,189,864
Bethnal Green	127,006	16,663	357,854
Newington (Surrey)	107,831	14,009	398,025
Camberwell	186,555	27,306	803,413
St. James', Westminster	29,865	3,018	666,813
Clerkenwell	69,019	7,129	326,709
Chelsea	88,101	11,380	465,353
Kensington	162,924	20,103	1,648,187
St. Luke's, Middlesex	46,847	4,813	278.313
St. George the Martyr, Southwark	58,652	6,766	237,042
Bermondsey	86,602	11,024	377,318
St. George's-in-the-East	47,011	5,815	199,237
St. Martin's-in-the-Fields	17,447	1,745	382,721
Mile End Old Town	105,573	14,047	335,344
Woolwich	36,600	4,851	116,980
Rotherhithe	36,010	4,845	193,217
Hampstead	45,436	5,869	417,283
District Boards, under same Act:—			
Whitechapel	71,301	7,594	369,824
Westminster	59,837	6,196	599,237
Greenwich	131,264	19,785	617,252
Wandsworth	210,397	30,754	1,183,278
Hackney	186,400	27,503	942,240
St. Giles	45,257	3,968	358,418
Holborn	36,122	3,251	286.729
Strand	32,563	2,827	436,373
Fulham	114,811	16,355	545,854
Limehouse	58,500	8,012	318,469
Poplar	156,525	20,487	670,476
St. Saviour	28,628	3,436	304,786
Plumstead	63,664	10,026	326,440
Lewisham	71.702	11,534	528,307
St. Olave	11,974	1,455	204,795
The Charter House; Gray's Inn; the Close of the Collegiate Church of St. Peter; Inner Temple; Middle Temple; Lincoln's Inn; Staple Inn; and Furnival's Inn	1,151	182	89,293
Total	3,832,441	488,995	27,540,029

A few Copies still remain of

MUNICIPAL LONDON;

OR,

LONDON GOVERNMENT AS IT IS, AND LONDON UNDER A MUNICIPAL COUNCIL.

Royal 8vo., pp. 792.   Price 25s.

BY JOSEPH F. B. FIRTH, LL.B.

OPINIONS OF THE PRESS.

"No writer has hitherto brought to bear upon this great subject such sustained power and such complete mastery of an intricate question."—*Westminster Review.*

"A marvel of patient assiduity . . . a most valuable work which treats exhaustively of the whole question, and the accuracy of which may be safely relied upon."—*Fraser's Magazine.*

"Merits the place of honour among standard authorities . . . masterly, lucid, and comprehensive . . . of peculiar value to public men."—*Athenæum.*

"The Corporation of the City, the Metropolitan Board of Works, the Gas Companies, and the Water Companies, are one and all scourged by Mr. Firth with an indignant rhetoric that might remind a political student of the tone in which Mr. Bright used to heap his scorn and wrath on the bench of bishops."—*Pall Mall Gazette.*

"A perfect cyclopædia of information."—*Daily News.*

"An elaborate scheme which must sooner or later occupy the attention of some Ministry."—*Leeds Mercury.*

"If ever a great municipal reform is carried, we shall owe a debt of gratitude to the writer of this book. In the meantime we commend it as the most complete, searching, and valuable record of past misrule, and the most faithful guardian and guide to build up a London of future."—*Weekly Dispatch.*

"To Mr. Firth are due the hearty thanks of the community for the invaluable work he has put before the public—a work which is a monument of clear, concise, far-seeing logical industry."—*Lloyd's Weekly News.*

"We most heartily recommend it to all interested in the question. The labour which such a work entailed must have been enormous, and enough to discourage any ordinary writer. It does not deal in generalities, but enters into the minutest details of every question, and by a constant reference to authorities, establishes itself as a work which may be safely and confidently relied upon."—*The Examiner.*

"Mr. Firth has obtained a complete mastery of the very difficult subjects he has had to handle. . . . We are glad to observe that the sober duty of research and compilation has not blunted his sense of the ridiculous or thinned his vocabulary of vigorous epithets."—*Law Times.*

"A great indictment against the Corporation and the City Companies. . . . Almost too elaborate."—*Standard.*

"An indictment formidable in every way. . . . The charges are so grave, and supported by so much *prima facie* evidence, that they must be answered."—*Spectator.*

"The work commends itself to the earnest attention of every thinking Londoner to whose heart the cause of truth, right, justice, and good government is dear."—*Cambridge Chronicle.*

"The must comprehensive and complete work on Municipal London which has ever come under our notice . . . the labour and research must have been enormous."—*Western Daily Mercury.*

"The magnificent coolness with which, by a stroke of his pen, Mr. Firth disposes of vested rights and gigantic properties, is only equalled by the singular aptitude he displays for arranging the smallest details of the New Utopia."—*City Press.*

"I hope it may conduce to the purpose both of enlightening the public mind and of fixing general attention on a matter which has too long escaped it."—*The Right Hon. W. E. Gladstone,* 1876.

"Most acceptable, as coming at a time when the municipal government of London is beginning to excite public attention after a lethargy of twenty years."—*The Right Hon. Robert Lowe,* 1876.

"An admirable work which I earnestly commend to every member of this House interested in the reform of London Government."—*Speech of Lord Elcho in House of Commons, June,* 1876.

"Great labour and great ability devoted to a great cause."—*James Beal.*

LONDON: LONGMANS, GREEN, & CO., PATERNOSTER ROW.

www.ingramcontent.com/pod-product-compliance
Lightning Source LLC
Chambersburg PA
CBHW020112170426
43199CB00009B/499